Building Global by System

from start to scale

Global Edge Consulting Corp

This book is a work of fiction inspired by real-world technical experience. The practices, systems, and principles described are based on the author's professional background, but the characters, organizations, and events are either fictional or used in a fictionalized context. Any resemblance to actual persons, living or dead, or real organizations is purely coincidental.

First Edition

Hardcover ISBN : 978-1-0695793-1-7
Paperback ISBN : 978-1-0695793-4-8
E-Book ISBN : 978-1-0695793-2-4

Praise for Building Global by System

Sourabh, through his imaginative storytelling, has created an enjoyable read and an excellent tool to educate product teams on the importance of global design and the necessary building blocks to achieve success.
Tex Texin, Chief Globalization Architect, XenCraft

A refreshingly honest look at the messy, human side of going global. This book gives you both the frameworks and the emotional reality of what it takes to scale across borders, from assessments to empathy. A valuable read for anyone leading globalization from the inside.
Renato Beninatto, Author of The General Theory of the Translation Company

Sourabh Suri's Building Global by System is more than just a guide; it's a testament to his deep knowledge and passion for creating truly global products. He masterfully unpacks the 'how' of systematic globalization, offering real-world insights that only come from years of thoughtful leadership. An essential read for every team striving for global impact.
Saurabh Kavathekar, Engineering Leader, Software Globalization

Building Global by System is the essential guide for all technology leaders aiming to scale software for a global audience. More than a textbook on globalization, it tells a story that links culture with code, strategy with architecture, and human stories with technical depth. It turns the complexity of building truly global products into practical, actionable insights, proving that globalization isn't a checklist, but a system, and a mindset. A must-read for anyone ready to transform local ambition into global impact without losing their soul.
Madhu Sundaramurthy, Global HR Director Board Sponsor Global Community - Women in Localization, Vice-President South CITLoB

Foreword

By Anna N. Schlegel

It is a rare privilege in one's career to witness the evolution of a technologist into a true thought leader, someone who not only understands complex systems but also redefines how we think about building for the world. Sourabh Suri is one of those rare individuals.

I've had the honor of working with Sourabh for over a decade, first at NetApp, later at Procore Technologies, where he led internationalization strategy on my team. From the start, it was clear that Sourabh didn't just do the work, he approached every challenge with a thoughtful, systems-level mindset. His curiosity was relentless, his integrity unshakable, and his drive to make products feel truly native in every market was inspiring. In the past 3 years we have co-founded www.universalization.ai where we continue to innovate and work on our next patent.

Together, we co-created foundational approaches to internationalization and even pioneered prior art using AI to scan for i18n readiness, long before it became a trend. This kind of visionary applied thinking is Sourabh's hallmark.

What you'll find in this book goes far beyond frameworks and best practices. You'll find reflection, clarity, and purpose. The opening chapter captures it beautifully, globalization is not just a technical exercise; it is a deeply human one. It begins in quiet moments of questioning, in empathy, and in the courage to build for people we have not yet met.

Sourabh understands that going global is not about exporting features, it's about building belonging. His insights into cultural adaptability, emotional intelligence in system design, and the importance of cross-functional alignment are lessons every engineering leader should take to heart.

I am profoundly proud of him, and proud to have witnessed his growth firsthand. His voice is exactly what this industry needs: practical, principled, and full of heart.

Anna N. Schlegel
President and co-Founder | Women in Localization
co-Founder | Universalization.ai

To the visionaries who believe that technology has the power to build bridges, not walls. To those who innovate not for borders, but for boundless possibilities. This is for you.

Acknowledgments

This book is shaped by the collective experience of professionals working at the intersection of technology, localization, and globalization.

To the engineers, localization managers, product leaders, QA specialists, and globalization architects. Your work solving the complex challenges of building for a global audience laid the foundation for every idea in these pages. From multilingual systems to scalable workflows, your efforts make technology more inclusive and accessible.

I'm especially grateful to those who contribute so generously to the community through open-source, blogs, white papers, and conferences. Your knowledge-sharing has made this field more collaborative, resilient, and forward-thinking.

To the reviewers: Tex Texin, Saurabh Kavathekar, Madhu Sundarmurthy, Peter Reynolds, Olga Beregovaya and Renato Beninatto. Thank you for your honest feedback, insights, and encouragement throughout this journey.

To Narendra Sadineni, who mentored me early in my career, not just in understanding the domain, but in approaching it with clarity, structure and purpose.

To Anna, whose mentorship deepened my strategic thinking and helped me link innovation with impact.

To my family, whose love, patience, and belief in me have been my quiet strength throughout this journey. Our conversations, values, and shared moments grounded this book in something deeper than process: purpose.

And to Ritu, my wife and my constant, thank you for being the calm at the center of everything. You supported me through late nights and long drafts, created space for me to focus, and reminded me to see the human side of every system. This book may carry my name, but its spirit carries you.

Table of Contents

Prologue

I've always believed that change announces itself in whispers. It's the subtle tremor beneath your feet, the barely perceptible shift in the air, long before the storm breaks.

Before the email that shattered our world, before the dizzying roadmap presentations and the global strategy decks that would redefine everything, there was a quieter moment. An evening walk with my daughter, Kashika, as dusk bled across the sky. We weren't dissecting platforms or market penetration. We were talking about new schools, unfamiliar places, and the strange, unsettling chasm between leaving one home and desperately searching for the next.

We were preparing for a move to Canada. For our family, it meant new schools, unfamiliar streets, and learning to belong all over again. For me, it mirrored a shift at work, reshaping something familiar into an alien landscape.

"Do you think it'll feel like starting over?" she asked.

I remember the way she looked ahead, not at me, as if she was already imagining the future.

"Maybe," I said. "But maybe that's not such a bad thing."

That question, so simple, so personal, echoed louder than any meeting room conversation I'd had in months. Because at work, we were facing the same challenge. We were preparing to start over in some ways, to reimagine what we've built, so it could belong to people in places we hadn't yet touched.

It was a moment of reshaping how we think, design, and deliver, about understanding that globalization is not an upgrade, but a bare minimum.

With ShopSphere, we had reached a threshold. What we'd built so far had served us well, but the world was calling us to do more. To think broader. To act with empathy. To lead with systems that weren't just scalable, but adaptable. Culturally aware. Technically sound. Emotionally intelligent.

That transformation would test every part of us, not just our architecture, but our assumptions. Not just our process, but our purpose.

And so, while the real work began with a meeting and a mandate, the true beginning was here, in this small, quiet moment of reflection, where the personal and the professional intersected.

Because to go global isn't just to grow.

It's to listen, to unlearn, and to rebuild our decision.

Chapter 1: The Globalization Awakening

An Introduction to Globalization - The Spark of Expansion

Terms you need to know	
Term	**Definition**
Globalization (G11N)	The process of designing and operating products so they can function across multiple global markets.
Internationalization (I18N)	The technical preparation of software to support multiple languages, regions, and cultural norms.
Localization (L10N)	Adapting content and functionality to a specific language, culture, or region.
G11N vs. I18N vs. L10N	**G11N** is the strategy, **I18N** is the code and design readiness, and **L10N** is the regional adaptation. G11N = I18N + L10N

February 27, 2023

The calendar invite landed with a soft chime. Subject line: *Global Expansion: Immediate Focus.* That was it. No preamble. No body text. Just four words that carried a baggage of countless future decisions.

I stared at the screen. The coffee in my mug had gone cold. I hadn't noticed.

The company had reached a point where the world was no longer something we could look at from the sidelines. It was time to expand, to take ShopSphere - our flagship ecommerce platform - beyond the borders we had always known. The questions started swirling: could we do this? Could we scale at the pace the world was demanding?

I had been working at Comventra Logics (we simply called it Comventra) for several years, and ShopSphere was our flagship product, a sturdy e-commerce platform that had held its own in North America, like a dependable old car that never let you down…, until the day someone asked it to cross oceans.

It wasn't built to cross oceans, or even countries. In fact, it wasn't even built to cover a country with more than one language. ShopSphere was a great product that could only speak English.

The office lights buzzed. I stared at the screen, trying to think past the static in my head.

A few months back, we were at the dinner table: me, Ritu, and the kids. Ritu was picking cardamom pods out of her chai. Vihaan had spilled a bit of milk on the table. Again.

The move to Canada hung in the air like steam off the mugs. The papers were signed. The boxes were half-packed. But it still felt more like a story we were telling ourselves than something real.

That night, my father pulled me aside.

"You're going to juggle a lot," he said. "But the world moves forward. So must you. Growth doesn't wait for comfort. Step into the unknown, and grow through it."

I didn't say anything. Just nodded and took another sip.

But now, as I sat at my office desk, staring at the invite, the next question hung in the air: could we adapt fast enough to scale both the platform and our lives?

I wrestled the rising anxiety back down. There was still work to do. “Can we handle this?” I muttered under my breath, though I wasn't sure who I was asking. Myself? Or maybe the silence of the office.

“Sourabh, you've seen the invite?” Lorenzo Santoro, our Chief Product Officer, stood in the doorway, his usual confident posture slightly tensed, like a sailor sensing a change in the wind. A stack of papers rustled in his hands, a paper trail of possibilities.

I nodded. Lorenzo is a forward-thinker but, like me, a little bit cautious about change.

“I guess it's time,” My voice betrayed me. Excitement tangled with unease. “Time to go global.”

“True globalization's more than just markets,” I thought. “It's a platform that works everywhere, no manual needed. One that gets context, adapts fast, and never makes a user feel like they're secondary. No matter where they are or what language they speak.”

Lorenzo dropped into the chair across from me, papers rustling in his hands. “We need a roadmap,” he said, breaking my chain of thoughts. “We've been talking markets for months, but now it's real. The business case is solid, but the tech side? That's a mess waiting to happen.”

I paused, letting the thought of going global settle. *“The benefits are obvious. More reach. New markets. Tailored solutions. ShopSphere's going global, and if we do it right, it'll thrive.*
This isn't just about adding customers. It's about transforming everything: every department, every line of code, every customer touchpoint. It's a massive shift. But it has got the chance to lead.”

I couldn't help a small smile. “A mess, huh? That's one way to put it.”

“Let's start with the basics,” Lorenzo continued. “Our platform's good. It works in North America. But translating that to a global scale? When we think of going global, we have to account for language, geography, money, personal habits, and the rules that govern each place.

We'll need to address all of that if we want to stay relevant.”

“We’re not starting from zero,” I said. “ShopSphere already has users in places like Singapore, Germany, even Brazil. But they’re adapting to us, not the other way around.”

Lorenzo exhaled, almost laughing. “Yeah, we’ve technically got a global footprint, just not a global experience. Our screens speak English, our timestamps speak American, and our checkout flow assumes everyone has a ZIP code.”

“Exactly,” I said. “It’s time we make it adaptable.”

The AC was steady, but my gut had turned cold. I could sense the gravity of the task settling on my shoulders. I couldn't just sit back and let others handle it. This was our future, Comventra's and mine.

The silence hung heavy between us. Mustering a sense of resolve, I asked, 'So where do we even begin?'

“We need to start by understanding where we are today,” Lorenzo said, setting his pen down. “Not just in terms of features and functions, but in how ready we are to think globally. What's adaptable, what's rigid, and where are the blind spots we haven't noticed yet?”

“You mean like a baseline check?” I asked, intrigued.

"Right," he nodded. "But broader than just the product. It's about our mindset, too. Are we designing only for the familiar, or are we open to the unfamiliar? Going global means uncovering assumptions we didn't even realize we were making."

I sat back, letting it land. We'd always built for what we knew, our customers, our markets, our rules. The idea of designing for people halfway across the world? Bigger than I'd first imagined.

It made me think of the *Blue Ocean Strategy*, a concept introduced by W. Chan Kim and Renée Mauborgne. Instead of battling competitors in crowded markets, the idea was to chart new waters, where demand was waiting to be created. Globalization was a journey into markets we hadn't imagined, filled with unique potential.

Lorenzo kept going. "Engineering and product matter, sure. But so do the rest: marketing, legal, support, design. If one team's out of sync, the whole thing stumbles. This isn't just a feature push. It's a mindset shift. Company-wide."

The scale of it hit me again. "So, we are fundamentally changing our business operations."

"Right," Lorenzo agreed. "But there's more. Globalization is as much about cultural relevance and emotional impact as it is about market expansion. We can't simply translate text and call it a day. If we want to build loyalty in new markets, we need to offer something that feels authentic to each customer's world."

I confirmed with a slow nod. "So, we're talking about empathy. About understanding what makes a customer in Tokyo feel seen and valued, just as much as one in Toronto."

"Exactly," Lorenzo said with a small smile. "Globalization, when done well, is a blend of precision and humanity. It's about designing experiences that are both scalable and personal, no matter where in the world they land."

Finding Ground in Uncertainty

I exhaled, a steady determination settling in. The realization hit me hard. Success meant crafting an experience so seamless, it felt like it was designed locally, no matter the geography.

Lost in thought, I found myself scrolling absentmindedly through my browser with LinkedIn open in front of me. My fingers moved without purpose, but then, almost as if by fate, a familiar name appeared in my feed. Naren. My old boss. My first mentor. The guy who taught me how to slow down and think, how to push harder when the path wasn't clear. The face in the photo had aged, more gray, deeper lines, but it was him. No mistaking it.

I needed guidance. Deep down, I knew he was the one who could give it to me.

But there it was: the hesitation. The question that kept running through my mind: Would he even remember me? It had been far too long since I last reached out. Too many years had passed without so much as a "hello." I was afraid of intruding on his life. Hadn't I moved on from the place he had once helped me navigate? Wasn't I supposed to be the one with all the answers now?

I drove home with the thought circling like a vulture - unanswered. It trailed me inside, settled in the corners of the house, refused to shut up. I tried to shake it. No use.

The indecision sat heavy, like a sack I couldn't shrug off. In my head, Naren's voice cut through the noise: *"Don't wait*

for perfection. Just do it." That line had gotten me through tight spots before: first launch, first promotion, first time leading a team.
Now here I was again. Another edge. Same fear.

I found myself scrolling through his profile again, almost by accident, searching for something, anything that gave me a reason to reach out. But of course, there was nothing. Just his professional accolades, his impressive career, and a steady stream of congratulations from colleagues and peers.

My mind spun. What if he doesn't remember me? What if this message went unanswered, leaving me staring at a blank screen, feeling like a fool? What if he thought I was reaching out just because I was struggling? I wasn't sure I could handle his judgment, not from someone whose opinion meant so much.

I stared at the message like it might bite. Still hadn't hit send. My finger hovered, frozen by hesitation. I could architect complex systems to connect continents, yet here I was, unable to bridge the gap of a few years with a simple message to Naren.

Before I could second-guess it, I was already opening LinkedIn. And I tapped on Naren's name. His profile loaded in front of me, and I felt the gravity of the moment. A message from me would be a reminder of how much I owed him. I felt vulnerable, exposed.

Then, in a strange moment of clarity, I remembered something my father had told me when I was still weighing the pros and cons of moving to Canada: *"People who care never truly disappear from your life. If their presence was meant to guide you once, it will do so again, no matter the years in between."*

I let that thought settle in, and with a quick exhale, I typed out the first line:

“Hey Naren, I hope you're well.” Then a few more lines, “It's been a while since we last spoke. I'm leading a major global expansion effort at Comventra Logics and would really value your advice. Would love to catch up if you have time.”

I hesitated, finger hovering. My chest tightened, heart racing. But beneath the tension, there was relief. Finally, a decision. For the first time in a long while, I wasn't standing still anymore.

With a deep breath, I hit send.

Immediate regret. What if he doesn't see it? What if he's not active on LinkedIn anymore? What if he doesn't even remember me? My mind raced through a thousand possibilities, each one worse than the last.

I sat back, staring at the screen.

No reply came. Not even a read receipt.

The screen remained unchanged, despite my intense gaze upon it.

But it didn't.

Whether Naren would respond, offering the desperately needed guidance, remained uncertain. And that was a thought I couldn't shake.

My Diary Notes

- Globalization is a company-wide transformation, beyond a technical strategy.

- Effective localization requires empathy, understanding the emotional journey of customers, not just their language.

- Scaling globally involves more than translation; it's about adapting to regional needs.

- Global expansion is a team effort, requiring collaboration across the entire organization.

- while technical solutions are vital, cultural adaptation is key to success in new markets.

- A well-crafted roadmap prepares you for the unknown, helping turn challenges into growth opportunities.

Chapter 2: Globalization Assessment

A Deep Dive

My company gave me a title and it sounded good on paper: Lead, Global Expansion. It had weight. It came with meetings, visibility, and the kind of quiet nods that suggested trust. But in the days that followed the announcement, something else crept in: the fear that I might not pull it off. Not because I didn't want to, but because I didn't know where to start.
I kept my notebook full, my calendar tighter. I did everything to look like a man with a roadmap. Inside, I was scrambling. Googling globalization frameworks between Zoom calls, pretending I understood things I was barely grasping.

There was no blueprint, no global playbook tucked in a shared drive somewhere. Just a vague mandate to "make the product work globally" and the unspoken assumption that I knew what that meant. I didn't. And if I failed, if we shipped something broken, or missed the mark entirely, it wouldn't just be my career that took the hit. It would be the whole team, maybe the company. That was the part that kept me up at night.

March 6, 2023

Just when I had almost given up hope of hearing back, a message from Naren on LinkedIn. Finally. Relief and excitement surged as I read his message. We quickly exchanged numbers and had a time on the calendar.

When we finally connected, it felt as if we'd spoken just last week. We exchanged life and work updates. He told me that he was on a trip to Everest base, which explained the radio silence. And before long, I asked if he'd mentor me. He agreed without hesitation, saying that while there were well-known aspects of the globalization journey, the real fun would be in uncovering the unknowns, those unexpected challenges that, once explored, would turn into some of the greatest learning opportunities. We decided on biweekly calls to start, a simple plan that already made me feel like I am getting a grip.

His words put me at ease. I didn't have a clear map yet, but the compass had stopped spinning. And more than that, I finally had company on the trail.

March 10, 2023

Minutes before the call, I was dealing with Kashika. She'd taken up tennis again after a five-year break, and the muscle memory wasn't cooperating. What once came naturally now looked foreign to her, and it was grinding her down. She'd come home after practice, silent, the sort of fatigue that didn't come from physical effort alone. She didn't say much, but as a father, I could see it in her eyes: frustration, doubt, maybe even regret.

Ritu was neck-deep in her new role with a local NGO. Meetings, site visits, outreach, the whole nine yards. She was doing good work, no question, but it was wearing on her. The long days, the unfamiliar culture, the constant demands, they were catching up.

But I didn't have time to dwell on it. Not now. I had a team that needed me. Work that wouldn't wait. And a call with Naren that had been a long time coming.

Noon hit, and I logged into Google Meet. Naren was already there, waiting. Seeing his familiar face, now with a few more greys at the temples, on the screen instead of across the desk brought a rush of relief.

“Sourabh,” Naren greeted with his usual calm tone, “Good to see you again. How's everything on your side?”

“Things are moving, Naren. Just... a bit heavier than usual. Work, home, settling here, some days it feels like I'm treading water,” I said, the strain threading into my voice before I could rein it in.

“That sounds heavy,” he said simply, his tone making space rather than filling it. “Starting fresh somewhere new is a whole life reset. But you're managing, right?”

I gave a faint smile. “Doing my best. Some days feel like too much.”

“Well, there's no easy answer. It's like the work we're about to dive into. Look, Globalization is about processes, tech stacks, and people. It's about understanding the bigger picture. It all starts with a thorough assessment, Sourabh. That's the first step.”

I sat up straighter as my interest piqued. “Assessment? What do you mean exactly?”

Naren didn’t hesitate. “A globalization assessment is a structured evaluation of how ready your product is to go global: code, content, infrastructure, workflows, everything.”

I leaned back slightly, hesitant. “Is it really that important to do upfront? I mean… leadership’s already asking for visible progress. I’m not sure they’ll see assessment as *progress*.”

He didn’t flinch. “That’s a common trap. A lot of teams skip assessment for that exact reason. The ‘we’ll catch things as we go' mindset. The overconfidence that your current infrastructure can handle it. Or just the pressure to *do something* quickly."

"But here's the thing. Skipping the assessment doesn't save time. It just defers your problems until they're more expensive to fix."

He paused, letting the words settle. "Assessment might not look like action, but it's the most strategic move you'll make. It gives you truth. And truth gives you speed, just the kind that doesn't backfire later."

Then he leaned in slightly. "Let me ask you, say, you're scheduled for major surgery. What's the first thing the doctors do?"

I blinked. "Run tests, I guess. Bloodwork, vitals, that sort of thing?"

"That's right," he said. "Before they even touch a scalpel, they check everything, because if your system's not stable, surgery could make things worse, not better."

"Right, that makes sense."

"But those tests don't just flag what's wrong," he continued. "They also tell you what your body needs more of. Maybe you're low on hemoglobin. Maybe your heart's under strain. You're not just identifying risks, you're calibrating the care plan. Vitamins, medication, rest, timing; it's all part of preparing for the procedure."

I nodded slowly. "So the assessment gives you a full picture before you act. Not just what's broken, but what needs support."

“You’ve got it,” he said. “And globalization’s no different. An assessment tells you what shape your product’s in before you take it global. Where your code is fragile. Where your workflows break. Where assumptions are baked in too deep. You might be solid in infrastructure but weak in content strategy, or vice versa.”

“And it tells you what you’ll need to handle that,” I added. “Time, effort, skills, maybe even a few rewrites.”

“Precisely. And just as important, it helps you move forward based on facts, not gut instinct. A strong assessment gives you real signals, what’s working, what’s not. That way, the decisions you make aren’t just educated guesses. They’re data-driven decisions, grounded in evidence.” I was quiet for a moment. “So the first step isn’t to scale or expand or even fix. It’s just to know. To diagnose.”

“Now you're seeing it clearly.” He gave a small nod of approval.

“Yes. And that's what I want you to do, a globalization assessment of your product. We need to determine if your product is truly ready for a global journey. If it isn't, we need to figure out the gaps and start filling them. The health of the product, just like the health of a climber, needs to be top-notch.”

“Just don't make the mistake of thinking it's all or nothing,” Naren warned in his matter-of-fact tone.

I felt the edges of an answer just out of reach. “What do you mean?”

“Global readiness isn't binary,” he said. “Some parts might be in great shape; others might need a lot of work. The assessment isn't about passing or failing. It's about understanding where you are and what needs attention."

I asked, "So, should I start with a Globalization Assessment or Scoping?", my a polite nudge, a way to hint that maybe he'd skipped a step and jumped to assessment.

Naren leaned back, unbothered. "Scoping *is* often the first move," he said. "But in practice, a lot of it runs in parallel."

He gave it a beat, then added, "You can start scoping, sure, but it matures slowly. Stakeholders, market signals, all the external factors. That takes time."

He leaned in again, voice steady. "Assessment is different. It's internal. You already have access. Code, infrastructure, workflows. That's where you start moving now."

"Hmm".

"In fact," Naren said, his tone steady. "When you do an assessment without the scope in mind, it gives you the clearest, most honest picture of where you stand, no bias, no preconceived direction. But when you add scoping too soon, it can steer the assessment, sometimes pushing you to focus only on certain areas. It's like going for a health checkup and only testing your blood sugar, ignoring everything else. You might miss that critical blockage in your arteries."

"You know you're going global," he said. "So, you've already got a rough scope to base your objectives around."

I was ready to get concrete. "Makes sense. What exactly does this assessment involve? What are the key areas we should focus on?"

Naren smiled, clearly ready for this part. “Okay, here's where it gets interesting. Let me make this clear: the assessment isn't a box-checking exercise. It's something you'll come back to as things evolve. But there's a framework that'll give you a strong start. Keep it close.”

He shared his screen, and I started copying the key points into my notes.

“First thing… your code. For internationalization to work, it has to handle different languages, scripts, date formats, the whole deal. Start by checking for hardcoded strings, region-specific logic. That's usually where the cracks start to show.”

I interrupted, “So, you mean any place where the code is specifically tailored for one language, like English, needs to be identified and made adaptable?”

“Exactly. If your code isn't language-agnostic, it's going to cause problems. Stuff like dates or numbers needs to adapt based on the user's locale. You can't assume that all users will be using English date formats or currency systems.”

I took a mental note, then added, “Got it. We need to ensure flexibility in the code base. What about UI/UX?”

“Ah, that's the second point. User Interface and User Experience. Think of it, while we generally call it translation, localization is actually about making the user experience work across cultures. Different regions have different design standards. Even something as simple as color can have varied meanings. A layout that looks intuitive in the U.S. might not work in Japan, for instance.”

I nodded, beginning to see the complexity of the task. “So, we need to evaluate language as well as cultural relevance of the design?”

“Yes. And this is often one of the most overlooked aspects of localization. The visual hierarchy, the text alignment, and even the images you use. They all need to be assessed for cultural fit. For example, right-to-left languages like Arabic or Hebrew require their own layout considerations.”

“What about data structures?” I asked, feeling a bit more confident now.

“Good question. Your system needs to flex. If your data models can't handle wide character sets or long strings, you're going to hit a wall. And most apps built for just one language do.”

I nodded thoughtfully, tapping away at my keyboard. “So, this exercise will help me ensure the infrastructure is ready for diverse languages and cultural norms.”

“To some extent…, yes. And that's why the assessment isn't just a one-time task. It's an ongoing process that'll evolve with your product. After this initial assessment, you'll need to build a roadmap for how to address the gaps you find.”

I paused, feeling a growing sense of unease. “But Naren, this sounds like a massive undertaking. Refactoring the code, changing the database schemas, updating the UI... If we're talking about all this, won't it take forever to globalize the application? It feels like it could be monumental.”

“Totally get the impulse,” Naren said, shaking his head slightly. “But don't start fixing anything yet. It's not the time. Right now, just need to look around and see what's working, what's not. No action. Just awareness. We'll get to the hard part after that.”

I felt a bit of relief at that. It wasn't going to be all on me at once. There was a process.

"Okay, I get it now. Step one is just seeing the whole picture. We'll worry about fixing stuff later."

"Right," Naren nodded. "You can't build a real strategy until you've seen the full picture. That's what the assessment gives you, a way to plan smart without overcommitting."

I was starting to feel more grounded in the process. "So, we assess the code, UI/UX, and data structures, then prioritize what needs fixing first, and then create a timeline. Is that the plan?"

"Yes. And you'll want to ensure that each area, whether it's the code, design, or data, is ready for localization. Once the assessment is done, you'll be in a good position to create a phased approach for execution."

"Got it," I said, feeling a new sense of clarity. "This gives me a much clearer picture. I think I can start drafting an initial report based on these areas. But what about the team? Should I involve everyone in this process, or just a select few?"

"Good question," Naren said. "You'll need a cross-functional team: engineers, designers, data folks. Each brings a lens that matters. After all, globalization is a lot about understanding people."

I paused, still processing his advice. "How will I know which implementations are right for globalization and which aren't?"

Naren took a sip from the cup on this table, his expression thoughtful. "You can only find gaps with your evaluation when you have benchmarks of best practices to measure against. To evaluate effectively, you need to know what the right approach looks like. These best practices will guide you in assessing your progress."

I nodded, intrigued. “Hmmm, I got it. So, where do I start with that?”

“Educate yourself,” he encouraged. “Explore resources, read real-world case studies. And don’t hesitate to seek training from those who’ve done this before. People who’ve navigated the traps, made the mistakes, and figured out what actually works. That kind of insight? It can save you months of guessing,” Naren said. “It’ll sharpen your judgment, help you see what’s working, what’s noise, and where the ground is about to shift.”

I nodded, finally feeling a sense of direction. “Alright, I'll get started on this. Thanks for breaking it down for me, Naren. I feel more confident moving forward.”

“No problem, Sourabh,” Naren said, giving me a reassuring smile. “This is just the start. Once you've got the assessment down, the next step is mapping out your localization strategy. But don't rush it. The trick is spotting the gaps early so you can fix them before things get bigger.”

After the call, I stayed at my desk, eyes on the screen, letting the silence stretch. The path ahead was steep, but I had a framework now. Something solid to stand on.

- - -

That evening, after I finished with my notes from the call, I sat down with Kashika. She was still navigating the difficulties of returning to tennis after so long, but I wanted to share something that had clicked for me earlier in the day during my conversation with Naren. I told her, “Excelling in any sport is a bit like tackling a challenging project. You can't just dive in without first knowing where you stand, where the gaps are, and what aspects you need to improve.”

I could tell she was still wrestling with the weight of it all. "What do you mean, Dad?" she asked.

I continued, "First things first. Go and assess your readiness. Start with the fundamentals: watch tutorials, seek expert advice, and analyze professional matches. Identify key techniques- grip, stance, footwork, shot selection, and pinpoint areas for quick improvement. Focus on your serve; with dedicated practice, you can enhance it swiftly. Then, consider essential skills like volleys, forehand, backhand, and the like." I told her what Naren said, '*You can only find gaps with your evaluation when you have benchmarks of best practices to measure against. These best practices will guide you in assessing your progress.*' These benchmarks are crucial for mastering your game."

She paused, thinking for a moment. "So... I should just keep going, even if it's hard?"

"Yes. I think so," I said. "The way you approach this now, with curiosity, will help you when life gets harder. But remember, it's okay not to have all the answers right away. Just start uncovering the unknowns, one by one. Like I'm doing with my work, figuring out what needs to change and what's already good enough."

Kashika nodded slowly, uncertainty still flickering in her eyes, but I could see the gears beginning to turn. I hoped she'd find a way to use this mindset to navigate her challenges. In the meantime, I was beginning to feel like I was piecing together the larger framework for my own journey, at work and home.

As I sat back, reflecting on the day's conversations, both with Naren and with Kashika, I couldn't help but feel a sense of clarity starting to form. The idea of identifying the unknowns, whether in personal challenges or work projects, seemed to be the key to understanding how to move forward.

But my thoughts quickly turned back to the task at hand. There was a mountain to climb at work, and it was time to put some structure around it. The Globalization assessment - this was my Everest. It was about identifying the gaps and about planning how to tackle them. I needed a clear framework; something that would help me map out the roadblocks, show me how to measure progress, and prioritize tasks.

I pulled my notebook toward me, ready to jot down everything Naren and I had discussed and started to form a strategy.

Framework for i18n Assessment:

5-Lens i18n Assessment Framework

A comprehensive view to evaluate global readiness

1. **Product & Architecture Lens**

"Is the foundation globalization-ready?"

- **Review Existing Architecture**: assess tech stack and scalability for global markets
- **Identify Key Functionalities**: pinpoint features needing localization (payments, regional restrictions, scheduling, measurements, etc.)
- **Data Structures Review**: verify support for multiple languages, currencies, formats, and locale-based data (APIs, databases, file imports/exports)

2. **UI/UX & Cultural Lens**

"Is the user experience adaptable and culturally aware?"

- **Current Localization Status**: check for existing multilingual capabilities and gaps
- **User Interface Evaluation**: confirm adaptability for RTL languages, text expansion, and flexible layouts
- **Cultural Sensitivity Review**: evaluate images, colors, and symbols for cultural neutrality or appropriateness

[To learn more about Global User Interface, please refer Appendix II - Universal Design with Regional Flexibility]

3. **Code & Integration Lens**

"Is the codebase flexible and integration-friendly for i18n?"

- **Internationalization Compatibility**: detect hard-coded strings, improper concatenation, and locale-unfriendly patterns (date/time, currency)
- **External Libraries Assessment**: check if third-party libraries/APIs (e.g., payment gateways) are i18n compatible
- **Localization Enablement**: assess readiness for locale-specific translations, pluralization, date/time formats

4. **Workflow & Collaboration Lens**

"Are processes and team ownership globalization-ready?"

- **Testing & Quality Assurance**: evaluate testing strategy for localized content, including automation readiness
- **Deployment Strategy**: assess build and release pipelines for supporting multiple locales
- **Collaboration Models**: define ownership and responsibilities for development, testing, translation, and deployment phases

5. Resourcing, Phasing & Impact Lens

"Are effort, risks, dependencies, and rollout phases understood?"

- **Effort Assessment**: estimate work scope and resource allocation
- **Impact Analysis**: identify cross-functional dependencies, risks, and ripple effects of i18n changes
- **Incremental Globalization Strategy**: plan phased implementation (avoid all-at-once overhaul)

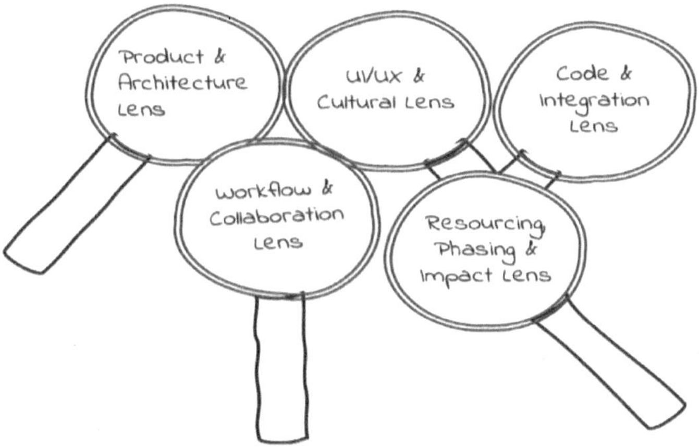

5 Lens - I18N Assessment Framework

[For a more detailed I18N Grading system, please refer to ***Appendix I*** *– Internationalization Grading System.]*

By the time I finished writing, I had a detailed map. Not a final destination, but a definite start. It gave me something to work with. Something that would guide my actions in the coming weeks and provide a measurable approach to assessing Globalization readiness.

I looked at the notes, knowing the framework was sound. But the bigger questions lingered. How long would it take? How deep would we have to cut? And how could we roll this out without blowing everything up in the process?

I also realized, this wouldn't be a solo climb.

To make this work, I'd need buy-in from product leads juggling launch calendars, infra teams deep in scalability bottlenecks, and compliance folks interpreting privacy laws in three languages. Most of them didn't even know globalization was on the roadmap, because technically, it wasn't.

The tech stack was only half the battle. The rest was people. And people had priorities.

If I couldn't align their goals with ours, no framework would save us.

As I closed my notebook, another thought lingered. This was just the beginning of the real work. I also need to form a tiger team to execute this exploratory work.

I looked at the half-empty cup of coffee in front of me. The liquid was cold now, the steam long gone. It felt like a silent companion to my thoughts. I hadn't even noticed how much time had passed as I was engrossed in the discussion with Naren, refining the framework in my mind.

I picked up the cup, studied it for a second, then dropped it in the trash. Done. Like the parts of the conversation, I couldn't answer yet.

The framework was solid. A step forward. But the rest? Still a maze.
How would we pull this off? What would break? How do we move without losing the thread?

No answers yet. But at least now, I had a place to start.

Naren had called assessments the foundation, but what if the foundation itself revealed cracks we weren't ready for? What if, as we dug deeper, the journey became more tangled, and the obstacles, more unexpected?

A shadow of unease crept in. Uncertainty hung in the air, whispering that something was about to shift, something I hadn't yet imagined.

We were ready to uncover every detail of ShopSphere.

The sheer magnitude of the work ahead sent a chill through me. My fingers curled into fists before I even realized it. I stood up, pacing, as if movement might disperse the dread knotting in my gut. I needed a magic wand, something to reduce this monumental task to manageable fractions.

My Diary Notes

- Assess Product Understanding: Review architecture, key functionalities, and data structures.

- UI/UX Assessment: Localization status, UI adaptability, cultural sensitivity.

- Code Review: i18n support, external libraries, l10n requirements.

- Workflow & Processes: QA, deployment strategy, collaboration models.

- Timeline & Resources: Estimate efforts, incremental globalization approach.

- Documentation & Reporting: Clear docs, regular checkpoints.

- Whether in life, sport, or the realm of software, transforming the unknown into the known is the key to mastery.

Chapter 3: Scoping For Globalization

Charting the Path Ahead

Terms you need to know

Term	Description
Localization Engineering	The discipline focused on adapting software for different languages and regions, often involving translation integration, locale-sensitive formatting, and infrastructure changes.
Encoding	How text is stored and understood by computers using numbers for each character
Hardcoded Strings	Strings embedded directly in source code rather than extracted for translation, making localization difficult and error prone.
UTF-8	A variable-width character encoding capable of encoding all valid Unicode code points, widely used for ensuring text compatibility across languages.
Unicode	A computing standard for consistent encoding and representation of text across different languages and scripts.
Pseudo-localization	A technique where readable but fake translations are inserted into the product to test how the UI handles different languages before real translations are ready.
Externalization	The process of separating user-visible content (like UI text) from the source code, usually by moving it into resource files.
White Labeling	The ability to rebrand software (e.g., logo, terms like "client" vs. "user") for use by different companies.

April 12, 2023

The assessment report was ready.

Weeks of discovery sessions, late-night system spelunking, and quiet Slack debates had finally crystallized into something whole. Every integration traced, every assumption challenged, every gap annotated in merciless detail. What started as a blur of scattered efforts had become a map, messy in places,

unfinished in others, but unmistakably a map. Timelines, architecture traces, localization red flags; all converged here, page after page. It didn't tell us what to do next, not exactly. But it showed us where we stood, and maybe more importantly, where we didn't.
Patterns had emerged. We had our truth.

This was the Tiger Team's biggest accomplishment.
Tiger Team, where Ava, Marco, and Nina had been assembled with care, each handpicked for what they brought to the table. Ava, with her knack for turning chaos into milestones, led the planning and project management. She was on loan from the Dashboard team, where she served as a Technical Project Manager. Marco with deep knowledge of the platform's codebase, especially the Micro Frontend layer, volunteered enthusiastically as a lead developer. And Nina, sharp-eyed and uncompromising, from the Recommender Systems team, offered her expertise without hesitation. She had been a localization engineer in the past. Together, they formed the backbone of our early efforts, with one clear mission: to assess, untangle, and prepare us for what came next.

It was everything we'd hoped for during those early conversations, yet instead of clarity, the report brought a new kind of dilemma: where to begin.
It didn't feel like the foot of a mountain anymore. It felt like a garden gone wild. Some paths were visible, others buried. A few things looked ready to grow, but plenty would need clearing first.
Before, we'd been fumbling in the dark, uncertain of what needed fixing. Now, with the light switched on, the sheer scope of what lay before us felt overwhelming.
At first, it just felt like minor tweaks. A schedule shift here, a requirement adjustment there. But the changes kept coming, and a quiet doubt started building. Something wasn't clicking.

As we dug deeper, the signs became harder to ignore. Simple things took longer than they should have. Ideas that made perfect sense in a slide deck unraveled when we tried to implement them.
It took a retrospective to point it out: this wasn't about fine-tuning anymore. Something at the foundation needed rethinking.

Everyone was pulling in different directions, prioritizing what felt urgent or technically intriguing. But there wasn't a real plan tying it all together.
It was a foggy day in Langley, where everything seemed muted and blurred. Yet the fog in the project was more frustrating than the one outside.
The conversation started innocently enough.
"We've already built some translation functionality," Marco began. "Should we push ahead with that?"
"Not yet," Nina interrupted. "The strings are still trapped in hardcoded cages. Translate what? Magic?"
Ava frowned as she added another bullet point to the whiteboard. "And what about database encoding? Marco, didn't you say UTF-8 issues might corrupt user comments in other languages? "
The discussion kept going for the full hour.
By the time we finished brainstorming, the board was packed with ideas- some critical, some exciting, and some downright impossible in the short term.
"What do we tackle first?" Ava asked.
Nobody said a word. The silence did all the talking. It was like a jigsaw dumped from the box. Every piece had a place in the final picture, but no one knew where to start.

That evening, I called Naren. After our first conversation, I started reaching out more often, and he'd begun to take a particular interest in helping me strategize. As I explained the chaos, he didn't sound surprised.

“You're dealing with misaligned scoping,” he said. “This happens when there's no clear path to delivering value.” “Okay,” I replied, pen in hand. “So where do we start?”

Naren gave a knowing nod. “You mentioned scoping a few days back, but we didn’t get a chance to really dig in. Let’s do that now.”

He leaned forward, elbows on the table. “I know you get what scoping is, 'drawing the boundaries before jumping into the real' work. But here’s how I picture it: it’s like sculpting. You start with a block of stone, and the real work is in chipping away everything that doesn’t belong. What’s left is what matters. Scoping does the same. It clears the clutter so we’re shaping the right solution, not just pounding on the whole slab.”

It made sense. Lately, it felt like I’d been swinging at the whole slab, hoping something meaningful would emerge. Maybe it was time to slow down, step back, and start carving with intent.

He broke my chain of thought when continued. “Scoping starts with three dimensions: User, Business, and Technical. These are interconnected spaces that you'll move between as you navigate the process.”

User Dimension

“For the User Dimension,” Naren began, “the biggest challenge is clarity. Too often, when teams scope requirements, they fill the list with wishful thinking, ideas that sound good but don't reflect the actual needs or behaviors of users across different markets and cultural contexts. Our job is to identify the tangible, high-impact requirements that directly affect the global readiness of your application, rather than accumulating low-priority features.”

He tapped a few keys, then looked back up, his eyes steady. “To get there, start with personas. These are detailed, realistic representations of your key user groups, grounded in research, not assumptions, and inclusive of users from different locales. A persona for a user in Germany may have very different expectations around privacy and formality than one in Japan or Brazil. Personas help flesh out who you're designing for, what their goals are, and what cultural facets shape their interactions. When you understand their motivations and limitations in each market, you can evaluate whether a requirement is genuinely valuable or just noise.”

“Next,” Naren continued, “map out user journeys. It's about the complete experience of a user interacting with your product, step by step, and how that experience might vary across regions. By charting how users navigate through your application, from onboarding to daily tasks, you'll spot friction points, gaps, and cultural sensitivities that a simple feature list won't reveal. For example, payment flows, date formats, address forms, or customer support expectations can all differ dramatically between countries.”

“And finally,” he added, “nothing beats observing real user interactions. Whether it's usability testing, interviews, or field studies, seeing how people actually use your product in different locales exposes the unexpected and confirms what truly matters. Sometimes what users say and what they do are different, especially when cultural communication styles are at play. That insight is gold.”

He sat back, his voice calm but firm. “If a feature doesn't solve a real problem for your users, wherever they are, it doesn't belong in your scope. That's how you stay anchored and globally relevant.

Naren laced his fingers together, his brows drawing together in focus as he finished his thoughts on user journeys and real interactions. His eyes searched mine for a brief moment, noticing the scribbles filling up my notebook, the slight furrow in my brow as I processed.
He tilted his head, his tone shifting from explanation to curiosity.
"Does that all add up so far?" he asked, his voice even and inviting. "Anything you're wondering about before we shift gears?"
Something about seeing real users, not assumptions, again brought reassurance. The path forward felt less tangled now.
"No, it's clear. Let's keep going."
Naren nodded, satisfied, and straightened up again. He clasped his hands loosely in front of him, as if gathering the next thread.

Business Dimension
For a second, Naren just stared at his notes, like the answer might be written somewhere in the margins. Then he looked up, slow and steady.

"Now let's talk about the Business Dimension," he said, pausing as he reached for his coffee mug. "This is where you step back from user interactions and ask: What does the business need to achieve? What's the strategic intent behind going global?"
I nodded slowly, already sensing where he was going, pen poised but not yet writing.
"You'll want to start by understanding the vision from leadership," Naren continued. "Engage directly with executives and key stakeholders. Their priorities set the boundaries, whether it's entering new markets, meeting compliance requirements, or strengthening regional partnerships. Without clarity, all those tactical tasks are just treadmill miles. High on effort but not taking you an inch forward."

He glanced up, meeting my eyes to make sure I was following. I gave a slight nod, underlining the word vision in my notes. "Next," he added, running a hand slowly down his jaw, contemplative, "you need to map how those business goals cascade down into tangible initiatives. Are we aiming for faster time to market in new locales? Are we trying to boost user acquisition in emerging regions? Or is it more about risk mitigation and legal compliance? Having that line of sight keeps your scoping relevant and anchored."

He paused, then added, "And don't forget competitive context. What are in-market competitors doing? Their moves shape user expectations and influence how quickly we need to move to gain market share or defend it. Sometimes, it's not just about what we *want* to do, but what we *must* do to stay relevant."
I exhaled, jotting quickly now as the shape of it became clearer.
Naren's smile returned, faint, but with that familiar spark of mentorship. "When you combine this with the User Dimension, you get a balanced view. What users expect, and what the business requires to succeed. Without either, your scope wobbles."
He let the words hang for a beat before reaching for his cup again, leaving me to digest the weight of what he'd just laid out.

Technical Dimension

As I jotted down a final note, Naren's eyes tracked the movement of my pen, then lifted back to mine with a small nod, as if to say, Ready for the next part?

He leaned forward slightly. "Let's move on to the third dimension, the Technical Dimension."

The pieces were connecting. “This is the part users don't usually see, right?” I said.

“Right,” he said, a spark of appreciation in his eyes. “It's the foundation that supports everything else. Content externalization, encoding support, scalable architecture for handling multiple locales, UI flexibility for text expansion or different input methods… all of that falls here.”

I weighed the idea for a moment. “So even though users don't notice it directly, it still shapes their experience?” “That's right,” Naren replied. “They don't see it, but they feel it if it's missing.”

“Without this groundwork, none of what we design for users or prioritize for the business will work globally the way we intend.”

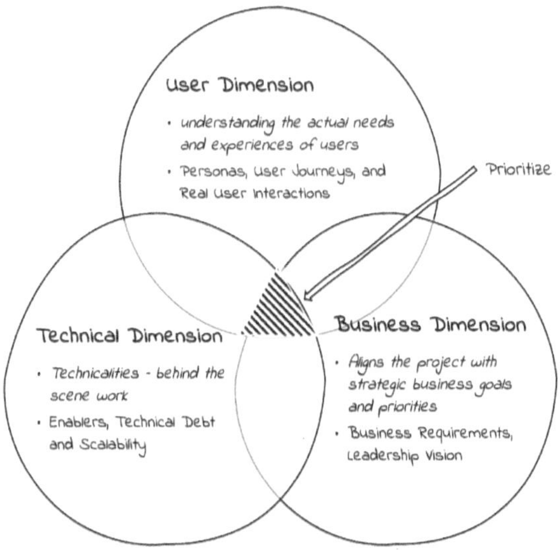

Three dimensions of Scoping for Globalization

Prioritizing

I nodded as I jotted a few notes, the three dimensions settling clearly in my mind now. But a lingering thought tugged at me.

“These are all solid ways to gather and validate requirements,” I said, looking up at Naren. “But once we have them, how do we know what to tackle first? How do we understand what really matters most?”

Naren's eyes brightened, as if he'd been hoping I'd ask. He adjusted his glasses.

“By taking an economic view,” he said.

Naren's explanation was methodical, but it didn't feel like a lecture. It felt like an exploration.

“It's about understanding which actions deliver the highest impact for the effort you spend. Sometimes that means saving users time or money right away. Other times, it's about clearing the bottlenecks that unlock everything else.”

“But, be careful here,” He glanced at me to make sure I was following, then continued. “ Making a feature truly available and usable means looking beyond the feature itself and considering all the supporting work around it. All the dependent work, the foundational tasks are absolutely necessary. That's what we call enablers.”

The term lingered in my thoughts, inviting a deeper look. “Enablers?” I echoed.

He nodded and began. “Let me ask you this: If you translated everything tomorrow, would it work perfectly for users in other countries?”

“Probably not,” I admitted. “We'd need to fix encoding issues, externalize hardcoded strings, and maybe even redesign the UI for cultural adaptability.”

“Okay,” Naren said. “Now think about this: Which are those tasks, without which the others become difficult or even impossible?”

“Or if I put it the other way round, which of those tasks enables the others? Which one, when solved, makes the rest easier or even possible?”

I thought for a moment. “Externalization, I suppose. Without it, we can't even start translating.”

“Right,” Naren nodded. “If you skipped that and jumped straight to translation, you wouldn't just be wasting the translator's engagement, you'd have nothing for the translators to work on. They'd be sitting idle, waiting for the externalization to happen before they could even begin.”

“So, externalization ‘enables' translation,” He continued, emphasizing the word ‘enables'.

“And let me tell you,” he said. “Externalization isn’t just about translation. Once you've decoupled your content from your code, you're ready for personalization.”

I looked up.

“Or even white labeling,” Naren said. “If your architecture allows it, enterprise clients can rebrand the interface, change ‘user’ to ‘client’ or ‘patient’ or whatever fits their domain. It’s a feature that wasn’t even on the roadmap, but suddenly it’s possible.”

“So yes, externalization ‘enables' translation, personalization, and white labeling. It's a true enabler in a real sense.”

Naren paused for a moment. After he noticed I was on the same page, he asked, “Now, let me ask you: If you've been putting in months of foundational work like externalization and your customers aren't noticing any changes, how do you think that affects their view of the project?”

I frowned, the implications swirling in my mind. “They'll probably feel frustrated or confused. If they don't see any tangible results, they might question whether we're making progress at all.”

“Absolutely,” he said, his tone steady. “Now, how can you ensure that the foundational work you're doing translates into visible benefits for the customers?”

I took a breath, considering his question carefully. “Maybe we could identify smaller milestones within the foundational work- things we can showcase to the customers while we continue the bigger tasks?”

“Good thinking. But you need to take the economic view,” Naren corrected gently. “You prioritize the features that will deliver the most impact at the right time, and not just work on their enablers, but also ensure everything else is in place: the translations, the readiness, the final delivery. The goal is to make the feature fully available to the user exactly when it's needed most. Also, you can run externalization and translations in parallel. When a sizable chunk of strings is externalized, send them for translation.”

He paused; his tone steady. “So, foundational work like externalization or switching to UTF-8 encoding doesn’t come cheap. It often touches large parts of the architecture. You might spend months laying this groundwork, and during that time, even domestic users may not see any visible product improvements. That's a risk. If you're not careful, teams can appear stagnant. So, while these enablers are critical, you also need to plan how to balance them with visible, incremental value, either by splitting workstreams or sequencing delivery intelligently."

I nodded slowly, beginning to see the framework he was laying out. "So, I should focus on delivering incremental updates that align with our foundational work, making sure customers see the value even if the full picture isn't complete yet?"

"Precisely. And remember, this economic view isn't just for the company's benefit; it's also about the users and customers of the software," Naren emphasized. "What are they going to gain in the next sprint that will enhance their experience? This perspective can help you prioritize features and improvements that resonate with them."

He leaned forward slightly, adding, "When you take that economic view, you're always working on the most important piece of work, the one that's actually demanded by the market or the situation. The goal is to address what truly matters now, not simply to release a feature for its own sake."

I considered this carefully. "So, for instance, if we implement robust time zone handling, users in different regions will immediately benefit from accurate local times, making their interactions smoother. Or by ensuring proper date formats, we can avoid confusion and enhance usability for customers from various locales."

"That's right," Naren replied, his enthusiasm evident. "Users should be able to connect the dots between your work and their experience in tangible ways to make it stick. When they see a connection, their confidence in you grows."

"Hmmm".

He continued, "You'll also need to validate every requirement. Ask yourselves: Does it actually solve something your users are struggling with? Is it even the right time to tackle it? And does it get you closer to what you're trying to achieve? Then, use a prioritization framework to decide what to tackle first. There's a simple way to sort through all this, MoSCoW. It's just Must-haves, Should-haves, Could-haves, and stuff you can skip for now. Keeps things clear so you're not wasting time on features no one's asking for.

Naren let out a slow breath, his smile warm with recollection. "You know, this reminds me of when I was packing for my Everest Base Camp trek. I stuffed my backpack with all sorts of things I thought would be useful: extra gear, gadgets, even a second pair of hiking poles. When the Sherpa saw it, he shook his head and said, 'All of this looks useful, but the mountain doesn't care what you're carrying. What matters is what weight you're willing to bear, and what it gives you in return."

He paused for effect.

I smiled, realizing once again that Naren hadn't just returned from Everest with memories. He seemed to have brought back a whole backpack of life lessons.

Unaware of my quiet admiration , he continued, "That stuck with me. It's exactly like prioritization in product work. Just because something can help doesn't mean it's worth the load. MoSCoW forces you to ask what's essential, what adds comfort, and what's just dead weight."

He continued, "Now, one tool you might find useful is the Kano model. It helps you separate the features that truly delight users from the ones they simply expect. That distinction matters more than you'd think. And when it comes to deciding what to build first, don't just go with your gut. Use something like weighted scoring, assign value to each item based on how much impact it'll have."

"These frameworks just help you cut through the noise. You'll know what to work on and when, no second-guessing."

We wrapped up the assessment conversation soon after, but our chat didn't end there. We drifted into stories, some about the project, others about life, and the quiet rhythm of shared purpose and easy camaraderie carried us through the rest of the hour.

April 13, 2023

The next morning, armed with Naren's insights, I convened a scoping meeting. Ava started by reviewing our goal: creating a global-ready application.

"Before we dive into tasks, let's take an economic view," I said, echoing Naren's words. "We need to figure out which pieces enable the rest and focus on those first."

We kicked off the scoping process with a core requirement: externalizing user-facing content - a foundational step for translation. However, we quickly realized that locale switching was just as critical, as it allowed us to validate externalization in real time. To streamline testing without waiting for actual translations, we decided to incorporate pseudo-localization early on.

As we refined our priorities, we turned to the scoping approaches like MoSCoW and Weighted Scoring to guide our decisions. These methods helped us distinguish between urgent tasks and those that could wait.

For instance, UTF-8 encoding emerged as a must-have. Without it, translations could be corrupted, impacting the entire globalization effort.

1. Value & Impact

- Does this deliver value soon enough? *(Quick wins vs. long-term impact?)*
- Who benefits the most from this change first: users, developers, or the business?
- Does this unlock immediate revenue potential, improve user experience, or reduce tech debt?

2. Dependencies & Enablement

- Does this enable other tasks or make future work easier?
- Are there foundational technical changes that need to happen before this?
- If we don't do this now, will it make future changes harder or more expensive?

3. Alignment with Business Goals

- Does this align with our overall globalization roadmap?
- Are we prioritizing the right regions, languages, or compliance needs based on business objectives?
- Are we balancing technical feasibility with business priorities effectively?

4. Risk & Side Effects

- Can changing this impact other features negatively?
- Are there downstream effects on integrations, third-party services, or analytics?
- What's the rollback or mitigation strategy if this goes wrong?

5. Business & Market Priorities

- Are there explicit business requirements that demand some features sooner? *(E.g., regulatory compliance, customer demand, expansion deadlines.)*
- Is there a clear "must-have" vs "nice-to-have" distinction for this task?
- What trade-offs are we making by prioritizing this now?

By the end, we'd categorized our requirements:

Must-Haves

- Externalize all user-facing content.
- Fix UTF-8 encoding issues in the database.

Should-Haves

- Implement locale-based formatting for dates and currencies.
- Build a basic translation pipeline.

Could-Haves

- Add region-specific UI themes.
- Support right-to-left languages.

Won't-Haves (Deferred)

- Payment modules for non-core markets.

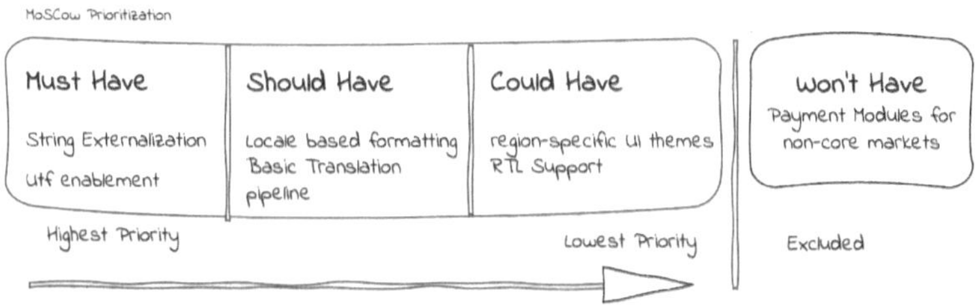

Naren's advice about enablers resonated throughout the discussion. Marco pointed out that fixing the UTF-8 encoding would simplify handshakes and data persistence. Nina added that externalizing content now would allow us to translate them later efficiently.

As the scoping meeting wrapped up, I glanced at the list on the whiteboard, each task clearly laid out with its value and effort. It felt like we'd finally carved out a clear path through the chaos, focusing on what actually mattered.

- - -

The following Saturday, I was trying to get through some emails in the living room when I overheard Ritu and Vihaan at the dining table. Vihaan had his math book open in front of him, but he wasn't really reading it. His pen kept tapping against the pages as if he were waiting for something to click.

Ritu looked over at him, softening her voice. “How's the studying going, Vihaan?”

"I'm trying to work through these fractions, Mom," Vihaan muttered, his voice trailing off. "There's this geometry test next week," he said, his voice tight, "and I don't even know if I'm gonna make it."

Ritu gave him a long look. "I'm glad you're tackling the fundamentals. But with geometry coming up, we'll have to figure out how to juggle both."

Vihaan threw himself back in his chair with a loud sigh, the math book slipping off his lap. "Yeah, but if I'm still stuck on fractions, how am I supposed to do geometry?" He let his gaze fall to the page, frustration clearly written all over his face. "It just feels like... too much."

"Okay," Ritu said, her voice calm but firm. "Let's work through this together. We'll figure out a plan."

Ritu suggested Vihaan spend 5-10 minutes daily on fraction practice to reinforce fundamentals without overwhelming himself. For geometry, she advised focusing on shapes, angles, and perimeter, concepts independent of fractions, dedicating an hour each day using worksheets and online resources.

Vihaan seemed more at ease as he considered the plan. "So, I can work on geometry without worrying about the fractions?"

"Exactly!" Ritu encouraged, "By focusing on geometry concepts that stand alone, you'll have the time to prepare thoroughly for your test."

"Okay, I'll try," Vihaan said, his voice a mix of determination and worry. "I want to be ready for the test... but I also kinda need to get these basics right."

As I sat there, I couldn't help but notice how his approach to tackling math felt eerily similar to my own struggles with work. Just as Vihaan needed to focus on his fundamentals while also showing progress in geometry, I, too, had to prioritize foundational work while delivering tangible results to our customers. This balance between efficiency and trust. Showing early progress would make our customers' lives easier from the beginning of the effort while ensuring that the application's globalization features become robust over time.

After dinner, I was still deep in my thoughts. The house had quieted down, the noise of the day settling into a stillness that only amplified my own uncertainty. I sat at my desk, staring at the assessment report one more time.

We knew what to work on now. We had the clarity that had been eluding us for weeks. And for the first time, I wasn't questioning the strategy.

But strategies don't execute themselves. And that's when I realized the new challenge was just beginning.

My Diary Notes:

- Enable the system by taking an economic view that goes beyond ROI.
- Ensure work creates value for everyone involved, not just the company.
- Validate every requirement to ensure alignment with goals and timely value.
- Prioritize tasks that enable other tasks to move the project forward.
- Balance fundamental tasks with progress to build trust and ensure long-term success.
- The MoSCoW framework ensures focus on critical features: Must have, Should have, Could have, and Won't have this time.
- Every organization scoping for Globalization has to do its own analysis. What is "must have" for us may not be for others.
- Use Kano analysis to identify features that truly enhance the user experience.

Chapter 4: Building The Team And Vendor Strategy

It takes a village

Terms you need to know

Term	Description
UTF-8 Migrations	Updating systems to use UTF-8, a character encoding that supports virtually all characters in every language.
Locale-ready functions	Programming practices that ensure software can adapt to regional settings like language, number format, currency, etc.
CI/CD Pipeline	Continuous Integration / Continuous Deployment: A set of practices that enable frequent, automated software updates.

April 24, 2023

I looked at the whiteboard, now crowded with diagrams and timelines from the previous discussions. The scoping phase was complete, and the tiger team had delivered admirably. But this was different. Execution demanded more - a team, a strategy, and, most importantly, alignment across the company.

"You know, the tiger team was great for assessment and scoping," Marco began, his voice steady, "but we need a dedicated team now. People who live and breathe i18n and l10n."

Nina, lounging back in her chair with a smirk, gave a theatrical nod. "I'm not against it, but building a full team means time, money, and caffeine we don't have. Scouting, interviews, onboarding... might as well add 'juggle flaming swords' to the to-do list." She looked pointedly at the sticky notes on the side wall.

Ava leaned forward, resting her chin on her interlaced fingers. "There's another option. Vendors. They bring speed and expertise. We don't have to reinvent the wheel."

"And lose control?" Marco shot back; his frustration evident. "How do we ensure quality if half the work is outsourced?"

The tension in the room was palpable. Each team member had valid points, and yet no clear path forward seemed to emerge.

Later that evening, I found myself on a call with Naren, seeking his advice. By this time, I had opened up to him again and didn't hesitate to call him ad hoc. I wasn't relying solely on our biweekly calls anymore. After listening patiently, he said, "This isn't uncommon, Sourabh. Execution always brings out the toughest questions. But here's what worked for me. Two strategies: build your core internal team and strategically engage vendors. You may need both to pull this off."

Before hanging up, he added, "And read *Truly Global* by Anna Schlegel. It'll give you a framework for what you're facing."

Intrigued by Naren's suggestion, I ordered the book on Amazon that very night. It arrived the next day, and I devoured it over the weekend. The insights were transformative. Schlegel made globalization actionable.

Her breakdown of team roles, vendor strategies, and cultural considerations felt like a roadmap tailored for Comventra. Every page seemed to address a challenge we were grappling with, from forming internal teams to building a trusted network of vendors.

When I closed the book on Sunday evening, I felt armed with a new perspective and a clearer sense of direction. This was about creating a foundation for sustainable globalization, which goes beyond mere execution.

Building the Right Team

May 2nd, 2023

The conference room felt charged, but not with tension. At least, not yet. Marco, Ava, Nina, and a few others were gathered, their faces displaying a mix of curiosity and mild apprehension. I stood near the whiteboard, waiting for everyone to settle.

“Let's get started,” I began. “As you know, the assessment phase is behind us. We've scoped the challenge, but now comes the hard part: execution. We need to build the right team, both internally and with vendors, to make this happen.”

I paused, drawing a circle on the board and labeling it **Team**. “I've been thinking a lot about this. And I also did some reading. Anna Schlegel's *Truly Global* had some interesting insights. But I'm not here to dictate; let's explore what might work for us.”

Ava edged closer, interest sharpening in her expression. “What does the book suggest?”

Key Roles

“Well,” I said, “The book emphasizes the importance of having a dedicated globalization team. Not just people moonlighting from their usual roles, but specialists. She outlined some key positions: a Globalization Group Manager to lead the effort, a Localization Project Manager for day-to-day execution, and a

Globalization Systems Architect to handle the technical infrastructure."

Scaling Smart

Marco nodded. "Makes sense. But that's a tall order. Are we talking about building this team from scratch?"

"Not necessarily," I said, drawing smaller circles around the main one. "Schlegel also talks about scaling. Start with core roles, then expand. For example, we'd eventually need leads for QA, architecture, and vendor management. But initially, we might combine some roles."

Nina tilted her head, twirling her pen like a detective with a hunch. "Hmmm, so, I can lead localization and be the QA gatekeeper both at the same time. Interesting," mild sarcasm in her tone. She continued, "This sounds ideal, but what about other roles? Where are we getting these people from? Are we hiring externally, or are we pulling from existing teams?"

Internal vs. External Talent

"That's the question," I said, looking at the team. "The book suggests avoiding inexperienced employees for critical globalization tasks. But we also can't ignore the resource constraints. What do you think?"

Ava was the first to speak. "I think we need a mix. Some roles, like the Globalization Group Manager, might need external expertise. But for others, we could train people internally, especially if they already know our systems."

"Training takes time," Marco interjected. "And it's about more than time, it's also about mindset. Not everyone is cut out for globalization work. How do we figure out who's a good fit?"

I nodded. “Good point. We should look for people with cross-functional experience and a global mindset. Training is inevitable, skills can be taught, but without the right mindset, they won't go far. That said, we need to invest in organizational health. It involves looking for talent that combines technical skills with creativity, communication abilities, and even psychology.”

“Psychology?” Nina asked, raising an eyebrow.

“Yes, psychology. Think about it,” I said to the team. “Globalization is all about understanding cultures, managing change, and sometimes navigating resistance. Having someone who understands the human side of things could be a good fit.”

Ava tapped her pen against her notebook. “Okay, but let's be real. How do we sell the budget? Some teams are stretched thin already.”

Budget and Buy-In

“That's going to be tricky,” I admitted. “But a centralized globalization model could work. If we spread the cost across departments, that expense them proportionally based on the usage and impact, and get the bare minimum for our team from the leadership, it may become easier to justify. Plus, we can argue that this team will benefit everyone in the long run.”

The room fell silent for a moment. I could see the gears turning in everyone's minds.

I turned to face them. “Before we move on, are there any questions or concerns about the team structure? Or anything you feel we haven't addressed yet?”

Ava glanced at Marco, then back at me. “Not a question, but… we need clear expectations. If we pull people internally, they must know this is a long-term commitment, not just another project."

"Totally," I said. "We'll need to communicate that from the start."

Marco folded his arms. "And we'll need to handle the inevitable pushback. Some teams won't want to lose their top performers to this effort. We'll have to tread carefully."

"No doubt about it," I replied. "We'll work on that messaging together. Anything else?"

When no one else spoke, I picked up the marker again and turned back to the board.

Engaging Vendors

"Well. Even with a well-structured internal team, we'd hit limits: of bandwidth, of expertise, of scale. That's where trusted vendors come in. Not as a crutch, but as an extension of our capabilities."

I circled the word Vendors on the board and turned to the group. "But... how we engage them matters. We need to be deliberate."

Ava raised her hand slightly. "So, are we thinking of handing over big chunks of work to vendors? Or just selective support?"

"Good question." I said. "Vendors can help us move faster and tap into the experience we don't have. But lean on them too much, and we lose visibility. Do too much ourselves, and we risk getting bogged down, spread too thin."

Marco sank into his chair, arms crossed. "Ah, so… it's about picking the right pieces to outsource, eh? What do we start with?"

"Hmmm, what do we start with?" I repeated, thinking, and then continued. "We'll need to evaluate which parts of globalization are tactical and which are strategic. In fact, we can think of the work as falling into three categories:" I noticed myself thinking loudly

"Strategic work is where we make architectural decisions, design systems, define integration points. That's the core of what makes our platform *ours*. It stays in-house, always.

Then there's **Tactical**, like translation services, testing, content QA. More operational, less technical, and easier to hand off completely.

And in between is **Pattern-Based Engineering**, tasks that are code-heavy but follow repeatable workflows. Think string externalization, UTF-enablement, or adding locale-ready functions. These are repeatable, sure, but they still demand expertise. Anyone can technically do them, but specialists who've done this before bring real value. They come with templates, mature processes, and a deeper understanding of edge cases. That's why these are great candidates for outsourcing, but *only* to vendors with real expertise in this space. If done right, we define the patterns, and they scale the execution with speed and consistency."

I glanced at the board and quickly drew a triangle, labeling the three points:

Strategic Architecture (Keep In-House)
Pattern-Based Engineering (Outsource with Experts)
Operational Localization (Outsource Fully)

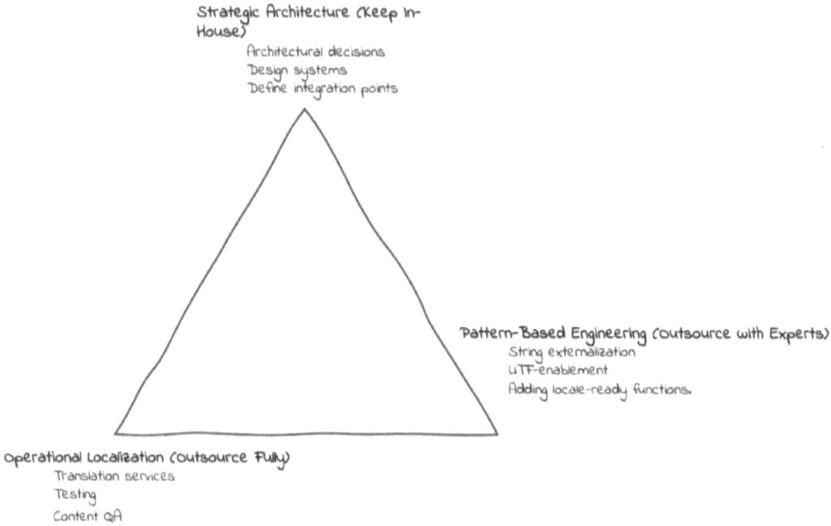

Nina nodded thoughtfully. “That makes sense. But how do we find the right vendors? I mean, there are dozens of translation agencies and localization providers out there. How do we know

who's a good fit?”

“Good question,” I said, underlining 'Trusted Vendors' on the board. “That's where vendor management becomes a key function. We need to build relationships with vendors we can trust, for their technical capabilities, and for their alignment with our goals. We can create a 'Vendor Manager' role specifically to handle this. Someone who ensures we're getting value, manages SLAs, conducts quarterly reviews, works with the procurement team, and even handles financial processes like invoicing and budgeting.”

Ava tilted her head. “That sounds like a full-time job.”

“It is,” I said. “But think about it. If vendors are handling a significant portion of our workload, we need someone to keep that process running smoothly. Otherwise, things can fall apart - missed deadlines, inconsistent quality, even spiraling costs."

Marco interjected, "Speaking of costs, how do we manage that? Vendors aren't cheap."

Vendor Engagement Models

"True," I nodded. "And that's where we need to be smart about engagement models. I was trying to understand vendor management a bit more and found some models, three main ones, each with its pros and cons."

I wrote the three models on the board: Consultancy, Time and Material, Managed Services, and Outcome-Based.

"This first one, **Consulting**," I said, circling it. "It's about bringing in specialists not to execute, but to guide. Think of it as buying expertise, not hands. You engage them to run workshops, train the teams, create checklists and templates, share best practices, or even validate your approach. It's short-term and strategic."

Marco leaned forward. "So, they don't build anything?"

"Yes. They help us make the right decisions so we can build things better ourselves or guide vendors to do it the right way. For example, we could bring in a consultant for a few weeks to help define our internationalization framework. It's not cheap, but the right guidance up front can save months of rework later."

Ava tilted her head. "And what about later. Like, once we're deep in the work?"

"Generally speaking, they come with the proposition of periodic checks," I said. " A quick checkpoint every few months or every milestone, to validate whether we're still aligned with the original direction, or if adjustments are needed. It gives us a safety net without slowing us down."

Ava nodded. "Got it. Consultants help us not repeat mistakes that others have already solved."

"Precisely," I said.

"Now, the second model is **Time and Material**. This model is flexible," I explained. "You pay vendors based on the hours they work or the materials they produce. It's great for evolving projects where the scope isn't fully defined yet."

Ava frowned. "Sounds like a blank check to me."

"It can be," I admitted. "That's the downside. The costs can spiral if we're not careful. But for short-term or experimental projects, it can make sense. For example, when we start localizing our platform for new markets like Southeast Asia, we might not fully understand the specific needs of those regions at the outset. We'll likely have to tweak the interface, adjust content, and work through language nuances. We may have to scale up and scale down the team frequently. A Time and Material approach would let us adapt as we go, without being locked into a rigid scope."

Ava nodded slowly. "So, it's good when the project's scope is still in flux, but you need to stay on top of it."

"Right," I said. "It's all about managing the scope to avoid runaway costs."

"This one," I pointed to where "Managed Services" was written on the board, "is for well-defined, ongoing needs. You pay a fixed fee for a set of services. It's predictable and stable."

"Sounds safer," Marco said. "But does that mean less control?"

"True," I said. "You get stability, but you might lose flexibility. For example, let's say we sign up a vendor to handle the ongoing maintenance of our backend infrastructure. The vendor takes care of patching, security updates, and system monitoring. But if we decide to scale our platform into a new market with specific technical requirements, like integrating with local payment gateways or supporting new compliance standards, we could find that the fixed service model doesn't easily accommodate these new needs. We might be stuck with a set of services that don't align with the changes we need."

"Now, this one is also interesting," I said, pointing to the last model. "Outcome-based. It's all about deliverables. You pay based on specific goals, like translating X number of words, achieving Y level of accuracy, building an international payment module, and setting up a CI/CD pipeline. Or meeting a specific deadline."

I sipped water from my bottle and continued, "The good thing is, we don't have to stress if it takes longer or needs more effort than we thought. The price is set up front, so there won't be any surprise costs."

"This sounds like a sweet deal," Nina said. "But doesn't it put a lot of pressure on defining everything upfront?"

"Correct," I said. "If we go this route, we'll need to be crystal clear about what we want. Otherwise, we risk serious misalignment. Say we bring in a vendor to help internationalize our platform for multi-currency support. If we don't clearly lay out what we need, like how to handle exchange rates, currency formatting, or regional taxes, they might build something that only ticks a few boxes. And by the time we realize it's not what we needed, we've lost both time and budget."

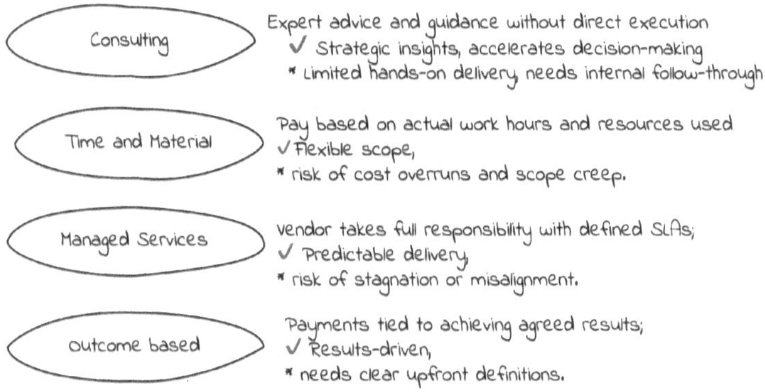

Deciding on the Model

I stepped back and looked at the board. "Alright, so here's the real question: which approach makes most sense to us?"

The room was quiet for a moment, and then Marco spoke up. "I think it depends on the phase of the project. Early on, we might need the flexibility of Time and Material. Later, as things stabilize, Managed Services could work for day-to-day localization. And for high-impact deliverables, like launching in a new market, Outcome-Based might be the way to go because the scope is finite and measurable, even if the work itself is technical. We can prepare the architecture, and ask the vendors to build the features accordingly."

Nina added, "We shouldn't forget consulting. They can guide us with initial training, help set up templates, and share practices we can build on."

Ava nodded. “I agree. A hybrid model gives us the best of all worlds. But we must manage it closely. Switching models mid-project could complicate things.”

“That's where the Vendor Manager comes in,” Marco said, looking at me as if for confirmation. “They'll help us navigate these transitions and ensure we're getting the most out of each model.”

Nina tapped her pen like a metronome. “What about pushback from internal teams? Some people might not like the idea of handing over proprietary workflows to outsiders.”

“We'll need to be transparent,” I said. “Explain why we're using vendors and how it benefits the company. And we'll keep the strategic work in-house, so no one feels like we're giving away the keys to the kingdom. And of course, we would sign NDAs with the vendors.”

I stepped back from the board, letting the team absorb everything. “I know, it's a lot,” I said. “But we don't have to figure it all out today. Let's just look at what's staring us in the face: what needs doing now, what we can't handle on our own, and what we're okay handing off. We'll build from there.”

The team nodded slowly. Some of the nerves were still there, but you could see it shift, like the idea was starting to make sense. This is how we were laying the groundwork for a strategy when it came to the idea of vendors.

After a pause, I added, “One more thing. While we've made significant progress today, this is not a decision we can finalize on our own. A strategy of this scale - building internal teams, engaging vendors, and choosing models requires buy-in from leadership. I'll take this to the higher management, lay out our approach, and do my best to make our case. Let's see how it goes.”

Ava leaned forward. “Do you think they'll approve?”

I hesitated, then said honestly, “Frankly, I don't know. Leadership's going to have their own take, different priorities, different pressures. But what we can do is present a thoughtful plan that addresses our challenges and aligns with the company's goals. From there, we'll adjust based on their feedback.”

With that, the meeting concluded. As the team began to file out, I could feel a mix of resolve and uncertainty in the air. We still had a long road ahead, with no promises of how it would all turn out. But we were ready to take the next step together.

May 7th, 2023

It was a quiet Sunday afternoon, perfect for a family ride along the Fort to Fort Trail, that scenic fourteen-kilometer stretch connecting the two Langley forts. Helmets ready, water bottles filled, we were just about to head out when Vihaan rolled his bike into the garage, his face a mix of frustration and hope.

“Papa, can you fix it?”

The front wheel wobbled. The chain was off. The brake pads squealed when I tried them. It wasn’t pretty.

I crouched down for a closer look: chain slipped, brake pads crooked, front wheel with a death wish. “Hmm,” I muttered. “This isn’t a quick fix.” I rolled up my sleeves like that might intimidate the bike into behaving.

As I started fiddling with the chain, Vihaan hovered beside me, full of questions.

“Why does this keep happening?”

“Can we fix it ourselves?”

“Shall we just take it to the shop?”

That last one made me pause.

He had a point. Sure, we could tighten the chain and pump the tires. Basic maintenance. But aligning brake calipers? Fixing a bent rim? These weren’t things I did often, or well. I didn’t have the tools, or frankly, the know-how to do it right.

“You’re right,” I told him. “Some fixes we can do here, like the chain. But if the wheel’s really bent or the brakes aren’t aligning properly, we’ll take it to someone who does this every day. We ride bikes. We don’t build or repair them. Some things are just better done by people who do this all the time.”

Later, as we finally hit the trail, I thought back to the meeting we’d had at work.

In the office, we were clear: the core engineering things like platform integration and architectural decisions, stayed in-house. That’s our craft. That’s what we do every day. But we brought in vendors for translation ops, testing automation, and localization QA (LQA), tasks others could do faster, better, and at scale.

At home, though, it was reversed. The bike? That wasn’t my domain. I was just a consumer. The repair shop was my “vendor,” and for good reason. They had the skills, the tools, and most importantly, the practice.

The lesson was humbling but clear: Core vs. context matters. What’s core to you may be tactical to someone else. And knowing when to fix it yourself , and when to hand it off, is what keeps both bikes and businesses moving forward.

My Diary Notes

- **Core Team + vendors** - Build an internal team & use vendors strategically. Both are key to globalization.

- **Key Roles** - Start with a Globalization Manager, Localization PM & Systems Architect. Expand later.

- **Vendor Manager** - Crucial for SLAs, reviews & finances. Ensures vendor value.

- **Engagement Models** - T&M (flexible), Managed (predictable), outcome-Based (incentive-driven). Hybrid works best.

- **Outsourcing** - Keep strategy in-house, outsource tactical work. Balance is key.

- **Transparency** - Teams should know why vendors are involved & how it helps.

- **Leadership Buy-In** - Secure leadership support for team & vendor strategy.

Chapter 5: Implementation And Execution Strategy

Where the 'Why' Meets the 'How'

Once we finalized our Team building and Vendor management plan, I set up a meeting with the leadership. My meeting went well. Though they couldn't allocate the full resources right away, they were supportive of starting small and expanding gradually. They asked us to begin with the immediate priorities and provided the assistance needed to bring in vendors, including engineers who could help with coding, integrations, and technical support.

For about a quarter, progress was steady but slow. The tiger team - Ava, Marco, and Nina had been pivotal during this phase, working across silos to assess our platform and refactor parts of the system. These steps laid a solid foundation, but we were still in the early stages of what was clearly shaping up to be a monumental effort.

Now, though, it was time for a shift. Leadership recognized that to move from strategy to execution, the effort needed full focus. Ava, Marco, and Nina were officially reassigned to the globalization initiative, giving them the bandwidth to dedicate themselves fully to the mission. It was a significant step, signaling the company's commitment to making this work. Alongside these familiar faces, we had a new addition to the team. We needed someone who could help us weave the various parts of the globalization puzzle together, someone who understood the entire process of internationalization and localization from a systems perspective.

That's when we brought in Amira, our new Globalization Architect. With 14 years of experience leading i18n and l10n strategies across Europe and the Middle East, and a recent move from Egypt to Canada, she brought exactly the systems expertise we needed.

She joined with quiet confidence, sharp in her observations, composed in her comments. Still, there was a certain formality in her posture, a polite distance in the way she engaged. During meetings, she'd flip through her notebook more than speak, her eyes flicking between speakers, as if still mapping the team's dynamics. No one said it aloud, but I sensed it too: this was a well-knit group, and she was the newcomer. The room wasn't cold, just… not warm yet.

We also began scouting for vendors to help accelerate our efforts, working closely with the organization's procurement team to evaluate our options. We considered several models based on the scope and needs of different tasks. For localization (L10N), a managed service seemed ideal, as it would provide a fixed, predictable cost for ongoing translation and adaptation work. For engineering and quality assurance (QA), especially with multilingual functionality, the time and material model appeared more flexible, allowing us to scale resources depending on the evolving needs of the testing phase. Finally, for more specialized tasks, like the internationalization of our payment gateway, an outcome-based model seemed promising, where we would pay only once the vendor successfully delivered a solution that met our goals, ensuring their incentives aligned with ours. And consulting was on the need basis.

Legal and finance were looped in early, helping us navigate contract structures, compliance risks, and cost forecasting. Their inputs shaped how we weighed each model, not just in terms of flexibility or incentives, but also long-term sustainability and regulatory coverage across different markets.

At least for the engineering work and QA, we managed to secure a vendor early - **LanguTrix**. With the vendor engineers now onboard, we had fresh technical expertise to draw on. These engineers brought invaluable experience with coding, integrations, testing, and resolving challenges specific to internationalization (i18n) projects. They became an extension of our internal team, accelerating progress and allowing us to tackle technical bottlenecks more effectively.

On the enablement front, we also engaged **LinguaLogic Partners**. Their team provided targeted training. They offered a long-term consulting model as well, but for now, we'd opted to keep the engagement light, focused on foundational guidance rather than embedded partnership.

Together, this group of seasoned internal leaders and skilled external partners formed the core team tasked with driving our i18n implementation forward. The pieces were finally coming together.

- - -

August 7th, 2023

The team gathered in for another meeting. Over the past few weeks, we had discussed the importance of i18n, the challenges of managing multiple languages, and how critical this step was for ShopSphere's future. But now, the conversation was about to turn to action. There was a clear sense that this moment was pivotal. Finalizing the strategy meant moving from theory to practice. And we were talking about internationalizing an existing application that wasn't internationalized by design.

I looked around the room. Each of my team members had their expertise, and today, they were taking the reins. I was here to observe, to ask a few questions, and to learn. After all, the real magic would happen when these brilliant minds started shaping this strategy into something executable.

Addressing Technical Dimension as a core

Ava stood near the whiteboard, marker in hand. "We've completed the assessment and identified several areas that need fixing. We also mapped those findings across the three key globalization dimensions: User, Technical, and Business. Each has its own weight, but for today, our focus is the *Technical* dimension. That's where the foundational changes will begin.

What Changes During i18n?

There was a brief pause before Marco leaned forward, his tone thoughtful.

"There's one question that's been bothering me for a while. Maybe it's too big to answer. Maybe not. But here it is: What exactly changes when we internationalize an app that already exists?"

Amira glanced up from her notes and added, "Well, one thing we often overlook when we discuss i18n is the architecture itself. It's much more than just adding language support or externalizing content. It's also about restructuring parts of the system to be more flexible and scalable, introducing new libraries or APIs to the architecture. For example, the way we handle dynamic content and the integration points, those need to be adjusted so they can easily accommodate multiple languages and regions without breaking functionality. The architecture has to be future-proof from the beginning."

Her point seemed to resonate with the group.

Nina, always quick to dive into the details, added, "Yes, and from a coding style perspective, we'll need to be writing more modular, cleaner code. For example, we won't be hardcoding strings into the app. Everything will be externalized into resource files, making it easier to handle new languages and regions. It'll also require us to adopt a more structured way of organizing the code."

Ava nodded in agreement. "Good point.

As the conversation deepened, a few of us began noting how some of these changes might intersect with other teams. Ava pointed out that product management would eventually need to rethink certain workflows based on regional preferences. I made a note to bring in support leads down the line; many of the challenges we were discussing, like error message clarity and dynamic content, would likely surface in their ticket data. It was clear that we couldn't design in a vacuum for long.

Ava started, "On top of that, there's the database schema. Right now, our tables might be designed for a single language, but with i18n, we need to adjust that. We might need additional columns for translations or even new tables for language-specific user data, such as custom labels, product descriptions, to name a few. Also, we'll have to make sure that our database can handle things like UTF-8 encoding to store characters from all the languages we support."

Marco chimed in, tapping his pen on the table. "And it's not just the backend. There's a whole rethinking of configurations too. We'll need configuration files that define what's available for each region. Things like which languages are enabled, what currencies are being used, what units are used for measurements, and which locale-specific rules apply."

Nina tilted her head, miming the act of rewriting specs midair with her finger. "Makes sense. This also touches the functional specs. Our specs might need to be rewritten to accommodate new requirements for each region. We need to think about how a feature behaves in different regions, which might change based on cultural preferences or regional laws."

Amira exhaled slowly, glancing out the window at a distant road sign. "And don't forget the knowledge base." She spoke with clarity, but one could sense she was still watching for cues, testing how far she could push her point without overstepping. There was the subtle wariness of a new voice entering an old conversation. " As we introduce new languages, we'll need documentation for all our teams - developers, QA, and support staff. Training materials will need to be updated, and we'll need clear guides on how to manage localization for every part of the app."

I asked, "So, in short, i18n is affecting the app's core structure, the way we write code, how we manage data, and even how we support users and document our processes."

Ava smiled, confirming what I'd guessed. "You're getting it. It's a holistic change. i18n impacts almost every layer of the application. Let's break it down a bit."

Ava quickly summarized the main points on the whiteboard:

1. **Architecture:** Adjusting the overall structure of the app to support multiple languages and regions.
2. **Coding Style:** Writing more modular and reusable code, especially around externalizing text and locale-specific logic.
3. **Database Schema:** Modifying the schema to handle multiple languages, adding new tables or columns, and ensuring proper encoding.

4. **Configurations:** Creating configuration files for regional settings like enabled languages, currencies, and locale-specific rules.
5. **Functional Specs:** Rewriting or adjusting functional specifications to accommodate region-specific needs and behavior.
6. **Knowledge Base:** Updating documentation and training materials for all teams involved in the process.

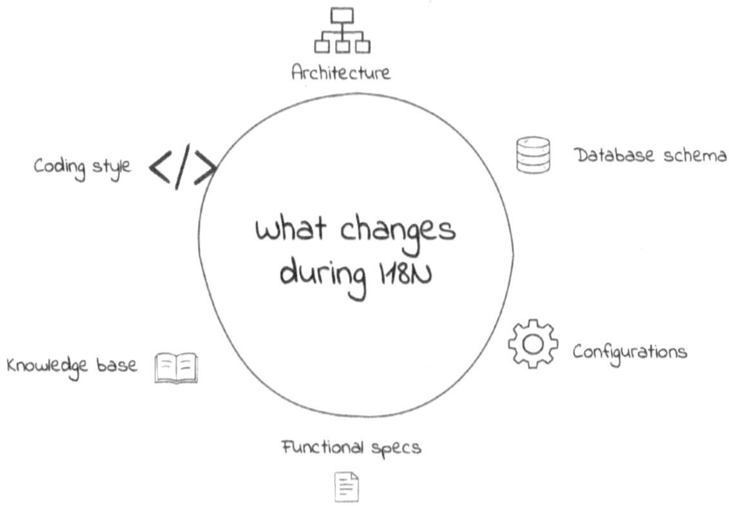

Execution Strategy Discussed

Ava glanced around the table. “Anything we missed?”

Marco thought for a moment. “Maybe testing, too. We'll need a comprehensive testing strategy to ensure that everything works as expected in each region and language.”

“Agreed,” Nina added. “Testing is 'must' at every stage to catch any issues early.”

I saw more than half of the room nodding.

Ava removed her glasses, rubbed her eyes, and broke the silence. “Alright, team. We already have the scope and priorities with us. We have also made a note of what generally changes during I18N, and now it's time to lock in our execution strategy. Where do we begin?”

Marco, who had been sketching out some notes on his laptop, was quick to respond. “I think the first decision we need to make is how we're going to handle text across languages. Specifically, the file structure and how we store it.”

Nina tossed her hair back with a quick flick, her eyes never leaving Marco's. “Right, we need a system that works across the board. Do we centralize the strings into a few large resource files, or do we go with a more modular approach and assign files per component or section of the app?”

Ava raised an eyebrow. “That's an interesting question. If we centralize everything, it could be easier to maintain initially, but it might also get a bit overwhelming as we scale. On the other hand, if we modularize the strings, each team could own their own parts, but that might lead to inconsistencies if we're not careful.”

Marco nodded. “Yeah, and there's also the issue of performance. Loading too many resources at once could slow down the app, but we don't want to end up with hundreds of small files either.”

I stayed quiet, letting them hash out the pros and cons. This was their decision to make. It was fascinating to see them work through these challenges.

Amira spoke up. “I think the modular approach could work best, at least in the beginning. We can have smaller resource files per component and load them dynamically when needed. It's a cleaner way to handle things as we scale."

Ava nodded, agreeing. "That's a good point, but we'll need a solid naming convention and some clear guidelines so that the resources stay organized. We don't want to end up with a mess of files that are hard to navigate."

"And we'll need to make sure we have a plan for adding new languages down the line," Marco added. "If we're starting modular, we should lay out how we'll handle new components and translation files in the future."

It was clear that they were all aligned on modularizing the strings for now. It wasn't the easiest option, but it felt like the most scalable. I made a mental note to follow up on how they'd implement naming conventions and organization, but for now, I let the discussion continue.

Amira continued, "And as we're planning our architecture, we must ensure that our localization pipeline can scale as we add new languages. From integration with third-party translation vendors to ensuring consistency across multiple teams, we need a streamlined, adaptable approach."

With the text management issue resolved, Ava turned to the next challenge. "Okay, moving on, what about the database? We can't forget about how we're going to store and retrieve multilingual data."

Marco was quick to bring up the issue. "We need to make sure we support UTF-8 encoding. That's non-negotiable if we're working with multiple languages."

Nina, always thorough. "Yeah, UTF-8 is the most universal option, but, uh,". She continued, mock-whispering this time like it was a conspiracy. "let's not forget about old data. We'll need a solid migration strategy to avoid breaking anything. We don't want our users to experience any issues when we roll this out."

I watched as Marco, Amira, and Ava discussed the logistics of updating the database schema and migrating the data. They were already talking about reaching out to the vendor for support. I didn't feel the need to interject. They had it well under control.

With the database discussion wrapping up, Ava turned her attention to the next challenge. "Now, what about formatting? Things like numbers, dates, and currencies are handled differently depending on the region."

Amira responded first. "Absolutely. We need an abstraction layer to manage libraries to handle those regional differences. That way, we don't have to deal with the intricacies of date formats or currency symbols every time we add new content or every time we decide to change the libraries in the background."

Marco added, "We'll need to make sure the system is flexible, too. As we expand to new markets, we'll have to adapt to even more complex regional settings."

Ava nodded. "Right, but we can't ignore the cultural distinctions, numbers, dates, colors, symbols, and layouts differ from one region to another. We need to build that into the design from the start."

Nina, always one to consider the user experience, spoke up. "We can create a set of design principles that apply universally but still leave room for cultural differences. We want to make sure our UI works seamlessly in both Japan and Germany, for example, but we don't want to compromise the user experience. That would also bring decoupling of locales, separating what's shown on screen, how formats behave, and how features function, so each can adapt independently to regional expectations."

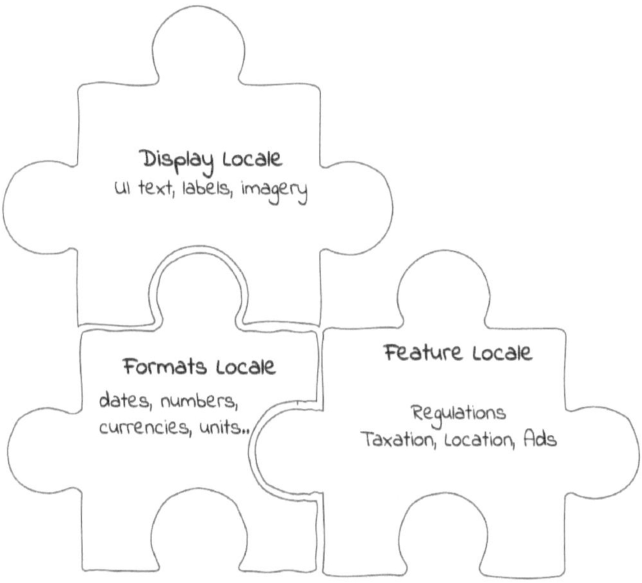

Locale Types

The discussion was deepening now, and I could sense the complexity of the task ahead. As they talked about UI considerations and the importance of being culturally sensitive, I reflected on how much I had learned just by being in the room. Not about code, but respecting people, cultures, and experiences.

As the team debated the pros and cons, I took a moment to jot down the key points. The consensus was beginning to take shape:

- **Centralization vs. Modularization**: A hybrid approach seemed ideal. Grouping related strings into moderately sized files to avoid the pitfalls of both extremes.
- **File Management**: Strict naming conventions and clear ownership would be essential to avoid duplication and maintain consistency.
- **Performance**: Lazy loading would mitigate potential slowdowns by ensuring only the necessary files were loaded per page or component.
- **Consistency**: A shared glossary and guidelines for translation would help maintain uniformity across the application.

Once these decisions were loosely sketched out, Ava shifted the conversation. "Alright, we've got a framework to work with. Before we wrap up, let's quickly discuss what we need to watch for during execution. Any red flags we should be aware of?"

Amira was the first to chime in. "One thing that comes to mind is edge cases. There could be functionalities that require special or custom treatment, which might deviate from the standard approaches we're planning to follow. While we should aim to minimize these, we must be prepared for some functionality that demands custom solutions. These will need to be well-documented and carefully tested to ensure they don't cause unexpected issues."

The room nodded collectively, acknowledging the importance of Amira's point. I made a mental note, impressed by how the team wasn't just sticking to the obvious concerns but diving into the fine-grained challenges that could arise. It was refreshing to see them considering aspects that could easily be overlooked, like edge cases that might need tailored solutions rather than cookie-cutter fixes.

Marco added, “Data corruption is another risk. If there's a mismatch in encoding or a translation exceeds expected limits, it could lead to errors or lost data.”

Ava nodded. “Good point. What else?”

“Data migration,” Nina continued. “When we're localizing existing content, we have to ensure that nothing gets lost or improperly mapped during the transition. This includes maintaining historical data integrity.”

“Regression,” Marco slid his laptop slightly aside, clearing space as he spoke with measured clarity. “Any time we touch existing functionality, there's a chance something breaks. We need thorough regression testing to make sure everything works as expected in all supported locales.”

Ava scribbled notes on her tablet. “Integrations and interoperability?” she prompted.

Nina nodded. “Absolutely. If our app interacts with external systems like payment gateways, APIs, or third-party tools, we need to ensure localized data doesn't cause unexpected issues.”

Then, Marco raised a point. “Since this platform wasn't built global by design, and it's still evolving, we need to make sure our changes don't break anything.”

I almost jumped in excitement. This was it. The moment that tied everything together. I was about to say something, but decided to remain silent, but my mind raced back to something Naren had said when we first started our mentorship. “Globalizing an existing application is like open-heart surgery. You can't stop it to operate it.”

Internationalizing an existing application is like performing an open-heart surgery. You can't stop it to operate it.

We weren't just adding features; we were fundamentally transforming the system while keeping it running. Every change had to be precise, every risk calculated.

But this was a massive topic on its own. Every point we had discussed today was critical, and trying to tackle everything in a single meeting would be overwhelming. We decided to schedule a separate session a month later, dedicated entirely to making globalization safe, without breaking what was already there.

Nina smiled. "Ok. Now the fun begins. Bringing it to life and ironing out the kinks."

I looked around at the team, impressed by their collaborative effort and clarity of thought. They had laid out a clear direction, and I felt confident in their ability to follow through.

Ava stood up, signaling the meeting's end. "Alright, everyone. Great work today. Let's get moving on this and regroup once we've got some progress to review."

As the discussion began to wind down, I jotted down the key points we had agreed upon:

- **Edge Cases:** Some functionalities might require custom solutions instead of standard approaches. While we aim to minimize these, certain features may demand unique treatment.
- **Data Corruption:** Ensuring translations don't exceed field limits or disrupt the integrity of existing data will be critical.

- **Data Migration Issues:** Moving data seamlessly into the new system without losing or altering anything is a priority.
- **Regression of Functionality:** We'll need robust testing to ensure existing features continue to work as expected post-internationalization.
- **Integration Issues:** Maintaining compatibility with third-party tools and APIs is non-negotiable.
- **Interoperability Challenges:** The application must handle varying data formats and standards across regions without breaking.

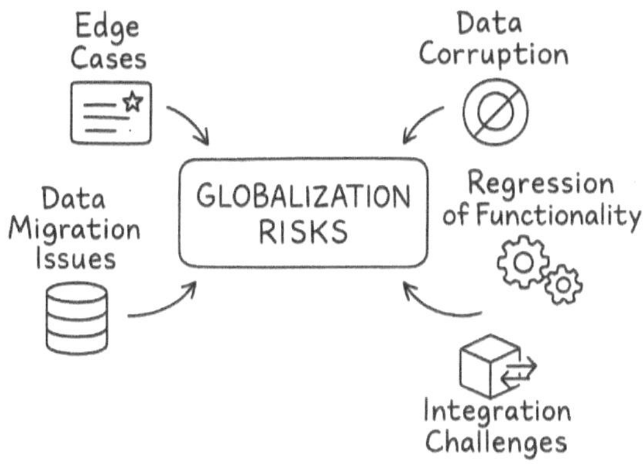

Finally, the team dispersed. I stayed behind for a moment to gather my thoughts. The discussions had been intense, and it was clear we had a long road ahead.

- - -

Finally, the last of the laundry was folded. I sank onto the couch, letting out a small sigh. A moment later, Ritu came in with two steaming mugs of chai, handed me one, and sat down quietly beside me.

“How was your day?” she asked, sipping her tea.

I was happy. “It was good. The team really took charge today. I hardly said a word, and they were all over it - discussing strategies, debating options, and figuring things out. Honestly, it was impressive to watch.”

Ritu raised an eyebrow, intrigued. “You're saying you didn't feel the need to step in?”

“Nope,” I replied. “I mean, I had ideas, but it was more interesting to see them figure it out as a team. I realized I don't always need to lead the charge.”

She nodded, a thoughtful look crossing her face. “Funny! That totally reminds me of this crazy thing that happened at work a while back. We were doing one of our community support events. Anyway, our project manager, this super organized person who basically held everything together, suddenly got really sick, like a whole week before this huge fundraising gala we had planned. We all thought it was doomed. But then, something amazing happened.”, Her eyes sparkling as she was reliving the day. “Everyone, from the volunteers to the admin staff, stepped up. The logistics team took over planning, the younger volunteers handled the social media campaign, and even the kitchen staff jumped in to create a menu for the donors. It turned out to be one of our best events, and we raised more funds than we expected.”

I looked at her, processing what she said. “So, you're saying it's not stepping back; it's making sure others know they can step forward when they need to.”

“Exactly,” Ritu said, smiling. “It's like a dance. You lead when you have to, but sometimes, letting others take the spotlight creates something even better.”

I got lost in thought. Maybe that was the real lesson from today. The strength of a team wasn't just in how it performed when you were leading. It was in how it thrived when you weren't.

My Diary Notes

- Globalizing an existing app feels like open-heart surgery - a complete overhaul of an application is needed while it is still evolving.
- Key i18n changes: architecture, coding style, database, configs, functional specs, and knowledge base.
- Red flags: edge cases, data corruption, migration issues, regressions, integrations, interoperability. Need a session on making globalization safe.
- Team working well together - sometimes, best to step back and let the collaboration flow.

Chapter 6: Safe Globalization

Globalization Without Breaking Things

Terms you need to know

Term	Definition
Linter	A tool that scans code for errors, bugs, and style violations without running the program.
Jira tickets	Tasks, bugs, or feature requests tracked in Jira, a project management tool commonly used in software development.
Hardcoded string comparisons	Logic in which fixed text values are embedded directly in code rather than externalized, often leading to failures when translations change.
Regular expressions (regex)	Sequences of characters used to define search patterns, which can fail with non-Latin scripts if assumptions like `[A-Za-z0-9]` are made.
Collation settings	Database configurations that determine how text is sorted and compared, which can cause mismatches if not adapted to multiple languages.
Pagination issues	Problems with data splitting across pages, often due to varying word or character lengths in different languages.
Traceability	The ability to track changes, decisions, or data lineage across systems, critical for debugging and compliance in global systems.
Interoperability issues	Failures in communication between systems or services, especially when regional data formats or standards conflict.
CI/CD pipelines	Continuous Integration/Continuous Deployment systems that automate code building, testing, and deployment.
Globalization Resilience Framework	A structured approach to building safeguards throughout the globalization lifecycle to prevent issues proactively.
Wrapper SDKs	Software packages that provide a simplified, standardized interface over other services or libraries, often used for internationalization.
CI/CD Layer	A framework layer that integrates i18n checks within automated pipelines to prevent bugs during deployments.

Terms you need to know	
Staging environments	Pre-production testing spaces that mirror the live environment to preview changes, including localized content.
Feature flags	Tools that allow selective enablement of features, facilitating safer rollouts and experimentation with regional features.
Rollback	Reverting an application to a previous stable version after a faulty deployment.
Hotfix	An urgent fix deployed quickly to address a critical issue in production.
Static code analysis	The examination of source code without executing it, used to catch issues like hardcoded strings or unsupported encodings.
Unit tests	Small, automated tests that validate the behavior of individual code units or functions.
E2E tests	End-to-end tests that validate the application flow, ensuring all systems and locales work together as expected.
TDD (Test-Driven Development) for i18n	A development methodology where tests are written before the internationalization code is implemented.
Lang attributes	HTML attributes that declare the language of content for accessibility tools like screen readers.
Screen reader texts	Text specifically provided for screen reader software to ensure accessible navigation and understanding.

August 29, 2023

That morning, I found myself meticulously arranging a tangled mess of paper clips on my desk, attempting to form a perfect spiral. It was an oddly satisfying distraction, a fleeting moment of control amid the chaos that had become our daily reality.

The checklist from that long January meeting with Naren had transformed into muscle memory. Our engineers, once overwhelmed by the weight of unfamiliarity, now moved with a quiet confidence. The linter rules barked less. The localization dashboard, once a graveyard of unapproved strings, now pulsed with green checkmarks. It was the kind of progress that made you believe that success was within reach. Still, something didn't sit right.

When I looked up at the screen flooded with Jira tickets, I found myself reflecting on our globalization journey so far. I couldn't help but acknowledge that this was far from a smooth ride. The idea of seamlessly adapting our application for a global audience had seemed ambitious yet achievable, but reality had its own way of humbling us. Our Jira board was inundated with regression bugs, and the firefighting had been relentless from the beginning. The core teams, along with our own localization and development teams, were stretched thin, scrambling to fix one issue after another.

Every one-on-one meeting with my team members had turned into a troubleshooting session. Ava, Marco, Nina, and Amira each had their share of grievances, frustrations, and war stories about the ongoing chaos. No meeting went by without discussing yet another unexpected failure or some edge case that had slipped through the cracks. Most of the time, we managed to pinpoint the root cause quickly, but implementation took its own time. And then there were issues that left us utterly perplexed, problems that seemed to emerge out of nowhere, forcing us to rely on trial and error.

The worst part? It felt like we were playing an endless game of whack-a-mole. The moment we resolved one bug, something else would break. Sometimes in the most unexpected places.

Whack a mole

Fixing UI rendering in one language would distort layouts in another. Adjusting date formats for different regions often led to broken calculations elsewhere. Hardcoded string comparisons failed when translations changed, and regular expressions failed when they didn't account for non-Latin scripts. APIs unexpectedly returned localized data, breaking parsing logic, and payment gateways failed due to mismatched currency formatting. These were just some of the issues we encountered, each adding to the mounting frustration.

The cycle was exhausting, and I knew that if we kept going this way, we would never stabilize the system. Frustration within the company was reaching a boiling point, so much so that some teams had even begun questioning whether internationalization was worth the trouble.

There were suggestions that we should abandon the effort altogether and focus solely on making the application work reliably in English. In our attempt to support multiple languages, we had unintentionally destabilized the application to the point where even the English version was no longer stable. It felt like we had done more harm than good, and that realization was a hard pill to swallow.

We already planned a meeting to talk about how to advance Globalization Engineering without breaking things in the coming week. By now, we had gathered a solid record of failures and pain points.

We needed a clear strategy. A proactive approach instead of the usual scramble. Ava and Amira had already been working with the team to analyze patterns in our issues and spot recurring trends. Their task was to bring structure to the chaos: organize the problems, uncover common root causes, and propose guardrails. We needed automation, stronger testing, smarter workflows, anything that could keep us from constantly cleaning up after breakages.

September 4, 2023

The meeting began with Ava setting the stage, addressing everyone in the room with a calm yet firm tone. She briefly outlined why we were gathered, emphasizing that we couldn't continue firefighting forever. “We need a sustainable approach,” she stated, before passing the floor to Amira.

Amira had come well-prepared. As she clicked to the first slide of her presentation, a structured plan began unfolding before us.

She started by categorizing the types of issues we were facing. “These are not internationalization or localization issues in themselves,” she clarified. “Rather, they are failures caused by the changes we've made to support i18n and l10n. These problems are affecting the very foundation of our application.”

Marco set his coffee mug aside, his attention sharpening. “So, are we talking about regression issues here?”

“Partly,” Amira nodded. “But it goes deeper than that. The system was originally built for a single language, and many underlying assumptions were never questioned. Now that we've introduced multilingual support, those assumptions are breaking down."

Nina chimed in. "Can you give some examples?"

Amira clicked to the next slide, glancing around the room before she spoke. "Let's start with the most common category - string comparisons failing due to translated content."

Marco rubbed his thumb against his jawline, brow furrowed. "What exactly do you mean? Are we talking about hardcoded strings?"

Amira nodded. "Think about it this way. When you localize content, two things change: the UI and the logic. UI changes are expected, but logic can break when it depends on specific words."

Marco tilted his head. "Like what?"

"Consider a simple condition: if (input === 'Yes'). That works fine in English, but what happens when 'Yes' is translated to 'Sí', 'Ja', or 'Oui'?"

Nina let out a breath. "The logic doesn't recognize the new words, so it fails."

"Exactly," Amira said. "What worked seamlessly before is suddenly broken just because the language changed."

Nina exhaled sharply. "The condition fails."

Amira nodded. "And suddenly, a piece of functionality that worked fine before stops working entirely."

Ava raised an eyebrow. "So, what's the workaround? Do we map every possible translation manually?"

"Not quite," Amira said. "We're not discussing individual fixes to specific problems right now. I'm focusing on identifying patterns. We already know the solutions. Our team has been addressing these issues. The real question is, how do we contain them to prevent build failures?"

She clicked to the next slide. "Now, let's talk about regular expressions. How many of you have written regex assuming only Latin characters?"

Marco groaned. "Guilty. What's the issue?"

Amira smirked. "Well, a lot of regex patterns are built with assumptions like [A-Za-z0-9]. Works fine for English. But what about Chinese characters? Arabic? Even accented letters in French?"

Marco ran a hand through his hair. "That means our regex-based validation could be rejecting perfectly valid inputs."

"Absolutely," Amira said. "If we don't define our patterns correctly, we block non-Latin languages without even realizing it."

Ava jotted something down. "So, we need to revisit our regex usage and make sure it supports multilingual inputs. Got it. What's next?"

Amira clicked again. "Validation errors due to locale-specific formats."

Nina sighed. "Let me guess. Date formats?"

"Bingo," Amira said. "If a form expects MM/DD/YYYY, it will reject DD/MM/YYYY, which is standard in Europe. The same goes for currency and address formats. What works in one country fails in another."

Ava tapped her pen on the table. "We should be detecting and adjusting formats dynamically instead of assuming a single standard."

"Thanks, Ava, that's exactly what I want to say," Amira said. "That's why we need flexible validation rules."

She switched to the next slide. "Now, onto database-related issues. Our database struggles in multiple ways when dealing with multiple languages."

"Such as?" Marco asked.

"Collation settings, for one," Amira said. "If we don't configure them properly, case-sensitive mismatches can happen. For example, searching for 'straße' in German won't match 'Strasse'."

Marco frowned. "That's just a simple search issue, though, right?"

"Not really," Amira said. "Because inefficient indexing strategies slow down localized queries. Some languages need full-text indexing, and others don't perform well with default settings."

Ava gestured toward the screen. "You also mentioned pagination issues?"

"Yes," Amira said. "Certain languages have longer characters, which affects how data splits across pages. If we don't account for that, pagination can break."

Nina looked thoughtful. “And schema changes?”

“If we don't design for multiple languages,” Amira explained, “we might run into storage constraints or retrieval inefficiencies. Storing and querying localized content needs proper planning.”

She clicked to the next slide. “Integration issues. External systems can cause just as many problems.”

Marco sighed. “I'm almost afraid to ask.”

Amira chuckled. “For starters, APIs sometimes return localized responses when we expect raw data. That breaks parsing logic.”

Ava winced. “That's painful.”

“It gets worse,” Amira continued. “Payment gateways can fail due to currency mismatches, causing transaction errors. And search and indexing functions can break if they don't account for locale-sensitive processing.”

Marco leaned back. “So basically, integrations need a layer of validation to ensure they're handling i18n correctly.”

“Precisely,” Amira agreed, moving to the next slide. “Interoperability issues. Problems arise when different systems try to communicate.”

Nina tilted her head. “Like encoding mismatches?”

“That's one example,” Amira said. “Some systems don't handle non-English characters well. Others have sorting algorithms that differ across locales, which can change the expected order of lists.”

Ava crossed her arms. "And let me guess. Cross-locale data exchanges?"

Amira pointed at her. "Correct. Misinterpretation of dates or numbers happens all the time. One system expects a comma as a decimal separator; another expects a period."

Marco exhaled. "We need to standardize our formats before data is exchanged."

"That would help," Amira said. "Finally, let's talk about deployment and configuration failures."

Nina rolled her eyes. "Are you talking about missing language files?"

"That's one," Amira said. "If the default locale isn't set properly, users might see missing text placeholders. CI/CD pipelines can fail if language files are missing. And auto-detection of locale? That can sometimes result in users seeing an unfamiliar language."

After going through these various issues, Amira sank back slightly, the gravity of the challenges evident on her face.

"So, what do we do about it?" Marco asked, already shifting towards solutions.

Nina was about to chime in when Amira held up her hand. "We're not talking about solutions yet. Right now, we need to understand the scope of the problem first. There are broadly five types of risks that existing applications have:"

She listed them out, counting on her fingers as she went:

"1 - Data Corruption"
"2 - Data Migration Issues"

"3 - Regression of Functionality"
"4 - Integration Issues"
"5 - Interoperability Issues"

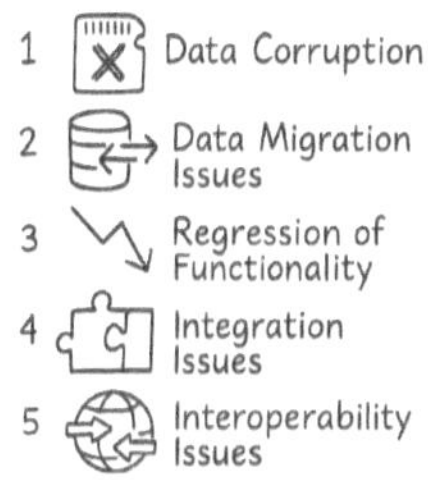

There was a moment of silence as everyone digested that. We were not only thinking of fixing bugs, but also of recognizing systemic weaknesses. That shift in perspective changed everything.

Amira clicked to the next slide; her voice steady but animated. "That's where the Globalization Resilience Framework comes in," she said, making eye contact with each of us. "Instead of reacting to problems after they've already caused damage, we integrate safeguards at every stage."

Amira clicked to the next slide. At the top, bold and clear, was the title:

Globalization Resilience Framework

She turned to the team. "This is what changes everything," she said. "Instead of reacting to problems after they've already caused damage, we integrate safeguards at every stage. Think of it as building earthquake-resistant buildings instead of fixing cracks after every tremor."

She gestured to the slide, breaking it down.

Pre-Build – Standards & Guidelines Layer
"This is where it all starts. We define best practices for internationalization upfront. No guesswork, no surprises. But just having rules isn't enough. We need engineers to understand why they matter. That's why we provide i18n training, so they know exactly why we ask them to code a certain way. If they see the bigger picture, why hardcoded strings break translations, why date formats can be a nightmare across locales, they're far more likely to get it right from the start."

She paused, letting that sink in before continuing.

"And we don't just leave it at training. We build playbooks - step-by-step guides that developers, designers, and even product managers can follow to make sure internationalization is done right. Think of them as blueprints for structuring code, managing translations, and handling things like text expansion or bidirectionality."

She clicked to the next part of the slide.

"We also provide standard libraries and wrapper SDKs, pre-approved tools that handle translations, locale formatting, and even things like pluralization. Instead of every developer reinventing the wheel, they can just plug in what's already built and tested. And for UI consistency, we've got pre-built components like date pickers, currency formatters, input fields that are i18n-ready from day one."

Amira turned to the group. "But standards don't mean much if no one follows them. That's why we have coding conventions, rules for naming translation keys, structuring locale files, and making sure no one sneaks in a hardcoded string. We also document Unicode and encoding best practices, because the last thing we want is garbled text showing up in production because of an encoding mismatch."

She glanced at Ava, the project manager. "And this isn't just a dev problem. Product and design teams need to be involved, too. We provide UX and design guidelines to make sure interfaces are flexible, layouts adapt, and text doesn't get cut off in different languages. Plus, we establish a process for linguistic and cultural QA, so we're not just translating words, we're making sure they make sense for the target audience."

Ava nodded in agreement, and Amira continued.

"Finally, this is all backed by cross-team collaboration frameworks. Localization teams have a direct feedback loop with engineering, and we conduct regular i18n reviews to catch issues before they snowball. It's about setting everyone up for success so when we scale to new markets, we're not scrambling to fix problems. We're ready from the start."

She took a step back. "The goal here isn't just to 'support other languages.' It's to build a global-ready product from day one. Without making it a painful afterthought."

Automation & CI/CD Layer

Amira clicked to the next slide. "Even with the best guidelines and training in place, we need a system that actively enforces them without relying on humans to remember everything. That's where automation comes in."

She glanced at the team. "Think about it. Would you rather catch an issue when it's just a few lines of code, or when it's already live in production, affecting thousands of users?"

A few people nodded.

"We automate i18n validation at every step of the build process. Every commit goes through a series of automated checks to ensure translations are complete, locale formatting is correct, and nothing breaks when switching languages. A controlled process to allow change in the database schema that would also include schema validations and migration testing to ensure database migrations don't corrupt locale-specific data. Even if a developer forgets to wrap a UI string in a localization function. The build fails, right there in CI/CD."

Marco raised an eyebrow. "So, we're blocking merges if a translation is missing?"

"That's what we should do," Amira said. "If a feature isn't properly localized, it doesn't move forward. No more 'we'll fix it later. And not only translations but all the other coding issues - calling noncompliant functions to format dates, numbers, and whatnot."

She clicked again, bringing up another point. "And we don't just check the code, we also run snapshot and visual regression tests. These catch UI issues like truncated text, broken layouts, and right-to-left rendering problems. We automate locale switching to test how different languages affect the design."

Nina chimed in, "I've seen some languages completely break a UI when the text expands."

"Exactly. And we're making sure that never makes it to production," Amira confirmed.

She took a step forward. "Now, let's talk about staging environments. We set up locale-specific test environments so we can preview UI changes in different languages before we deploy them. And when we roll out new translations, we don't release them to everyone at once. We use feature flags to test with a smaller group first. If anything looks off, we roll back instantly."

Ava nodded thoughtfully. "That makes sense. So instead of reacting to i18n bugs, we're catching them upfront and controlling how they get released?"

"That's the whole point. Prevent, don't fix." Amira said with a smile.

Amira clicked to the next slide. "Now, we come to the third layer: Monitoring & Testing. This is where we proactively catch localization issues before they impact users."

She pointed to the first bullet. "A/B testing plays a crucial role here."

"Let's say we're implementing a new way to detect user language. Should we rely on browser settings, IP address, or user preferences? Instead of rolling out a single method and hoping for the best, A/B testing lets us run multiple approaches at the same time and measure which one leads to the fewest user overrides. If users keep changing their language settings manually, that tells us we need to adjust our detection logic."

Marco adjusted his watch absentmindedly, his attention firmly on the conversation. "But what if we pick a method that works well in one country but causes issues elsewhere?"

Amira nodded. "Exactly! That's why A/B testing isn't just about picking one winner. We can segment users by region and see if different methods perform better in different markets. If IP-based detection works well in Europe but fails in Southeast Asia, we can adapt accordingly."

She clicked the next bullet. "Feature flags give us even more control."

"Instead of pushing new localization logic to everyone at once, we can enable it gradually for a small set of users. If something isn't working, we can turn it off instantly, without waiting for a new release. This means we can experiment, refine, and react quickly if anything breaks."

She turned back to the team. "By combining A/B testing and feature flags in this layer, we don't just react to localization issues, we prevent them from ever reaching users."

Amira took a step back and glanced at the team. "Even with all these layers in place, some issues will inevitably slip through and make it to production. That's why we need a robust system to detect, respond, and fix them - fast."

She clicked to the next slide. "This brings us to our final layer - Incident Recovery & Remediation."

"First, real-time alerts." She pointed at the screen. "We set up error monitoring to detect crashes, missing translations, encoding failures, basically, anything that breaks the user experience. But detecting is just step one. We also define clear escalation paths so that minor text glitches don't get the same urgency as, say, an incorrect currency format on a checkout page."

Marco raised an eyebrow. "And if something critical does break?"

"That's where rollback and hotfix mechanisms come in." Amira continued. "We use feature flags to disable faulty localization updates instantly. Gradual rollouts help us release changes in a controlled manner, minimizing risk. And if something still goes wrong, our deployment pipeline can automatically roll back failed updates."

She moved to the next point. "Debugging and forensics."

“Most of the time, it's not enough to know something broke. We need to understand why. That's where detailed logs come in, capturing locale, UI components, and even the translation keys involved. We can also use session replay techniques to see exactly what the user experienced, and feedback collection channels to gather real-world reports.”

Nina crossed her arms. “Okay, but what if it's a translation error that needs fixing immediately? Do we wait for the next deployment?”

Amira smiled. “Not necessarily. The key is agility. Some issues need immediate patching, while others can be prioritized for upcoming iterations.”

“If a translation is missing, we can show English instead of a broken placeholder as a temporary fallback. But for critical issues, like a mistranslated checkout button or legal disclaimers, we should have a way to push fixes instantly without waiting for a full deployment.”

She continued, “For everything else, we log and categorize the issues. If the impact is low, we slot them into the next planned iteration instead of reacting in real time. That way, we stay agile without overwhelming the team with constant hotfixes.”

She turned to the final point. “And last, but just as important: post-incident analysis.”

“Every major localization failure should lead to a lesson. Root cause analysis helps us fix process gaps, enhance test coverage for things like RTL layouts, and improve deployment safeguards so the same issue doesn't happen again.”

Amira closed the slide. “With this final layer, we're not just fixing problems. We're making sure they don't happen again.”

Amira clicked through the final slide and turned back to the room. “So, that's the framework. Four layers. Knowledge over guesswork. Prevention over reaction. Automation over manual fixes. Resilience over fragility. If we do this right, we’re creating a system designed to solve today’s challenges and stay resilient in the face of future ones.”

She crossed her arms, letting the weight of it settle. “The real question is: how do we start?”

A brief silence filled the room before Marco broke it. “Right. This all makes sense, but what's the first thing we change? Where do we even begin?”

Ava nodded. “Yeah, this is a lot. Do we roll it out in phases, or do we try to fix everything at once?”

I exhaled, already thinking ahead. “Good questions. We can't overhaul everything overnight. But we also can't keep firefighting with every release. We need a transition plan.”

I looked at Amira, and she gave a knowing smile. “Let's start small,” she said. “A pilot. We pick one upcoming feature and apply only the necessary rules from the framework. Nothing extra, nothing premature.”

Marco raised an eyebrow. “So, we're not drafting rules for everything all at once?”

“Yes,” Amira nodded. “If a feature doesn't involve currency, we're not wasting time defining rules for price rounding or conversion. If it doesn't deal with user-generated content, we don't need complex text direction handling. We establish rules as we need them, based on real use cases, not hypotheticals.”

Ava tapped her pen against the table. “That makes sense. We focus on what's relevant instead of creating a rulebook full of things we may never need.”

I nodded. “Right. And as we move forward, we refine. If we encounter a scenario that requires stricter handling, say, dynamic text layouts or high-impact transactional messages, then we bring in the additional rules. But we don't start with a hundred rules just for the sake of it.”

The energy in the room shifted.

I nodded. “A controlled experiment. That way, we don't just theorize. We prove it works.”

Ava jotted something down in her notebook. “Alright. Let's pick a feature and map out the steps. We'll regroup in a few days.”

I looked around the table, feeling something I hadn't had in a long time - momentum.

As the meeting wrapped up and people started gathering their things, I sank deeper into my chair, watching the team.

And for the first time since this whole globalization challenge began, I felt like we were taking control and not reacting.

I drew a rough diagram on my notepad, making the 'pre-build' the largest layer as most issues should be addressed at this level, and there should be just a few exceptions that would reach the 'Incident Recover & Recommendation' layer.

I could sense the shift. Less hesitation, more clarity. We had a starting point, a real plan. No over-engineering, no endless debates. Just a focused, pragmatic approach.

Now, it was time to put it to the test.

- - -

That evening, at home, things were far less structured. Vihaan was sprawled across the living room floor, building something elaborate with his Lego set, while Kashika sat at the dining table, earphones in, furiously typing away. Ritu was flipping through a magazine, occasionally glancing up at the kids with a knowing smile. It was one of those rare moments of quiet chaos, everyone lost in their own world, yet together. I leaned back, taking it all in. At work, I was mapping out layers of a framework. Here, life unfolded without one. And somehow, both needed their own kind of resilience.

My Diary Notes

When internationalizing an existing application, watch for:

- "Functionality Regression"
- Data Corruption
- Data Migration Issues
- Integration Issues
- Interoperability Issues

Layers in the Globalization Resilience Framework

- Pre-Build (Standards & Guidelines Layer) - Best practices, training, playbooks, and standard libraries
- Build & Deployment (Automation & CI/CD Layer) - Automated checks, translation coverage validation, and blocking rule violations

Fix the problem, but fortify against its return.

- Runtime (Monitoring & Testing Layer) - A/B testing, feature flags, and observability for inconsistencies
- Incident Recovery (Recovery & Remediation Layer) - Real-time alerts, rollback mechanisms, debugging tools, and post-incident analysis

Key Learning

Structure turns chaos into solvable steps.

Use what matters, when it matters. No more, no less.

Chapter 7: The Art And Science Of Localization

Not Lost in Translation

Terms you need to know	
Term	**Definition**
Concatenation	The practice of dynamically joining text strings in code (e.g., `"Hello " + name + "!"`). It's considered problematic for localization because different languages have varied grammar and word order, leading to ungrammatical or confusing translations.
Placeholders	A localization-friendly technique for embedding variables within a full sentence (e.g., `"The customer has {action} the order"`). This allows translators to maintain grammatical accuracy across languages by controlling sentence structure around the variable.
Pluralization	The process of adapting words based on quantity, which differs widely across languages. While English uses simple singular/plural forms (e.g., "apple/apples"), many languages have multiple plural categories or different rules entirely.
Grammatical Gender	A linguistic feature in many languages where nouns, pronouns, and adjectives change based on gender (e.g., masculine/feminine forms in French: *chanteur* vs. *chanteuse*). Handling this correctly in software often requires separate localized strings or logic to choose the appropriate form.

Oct 11, 2023

The email from Arjan landed in our team's distribution list while I was deep in the middle of drafting the latest project brief.

"Here we go again," I muttered, glancing at the subject line:

Subject: Localization Issues Observed – Need Guidance on Logging

Arjan was our in-country reviewer, someone testing our product as a real user in his region would. Unlike automated tests or internal QA, in-country reviewers catch issues that only emerge in real-world usage. It's the difference between a translation that technically works and one that actually feels right in a given culture.

His email was to the point, listing his observations without over-explaining:

> "While testing the new feature, I noticed quite a few linguistic and formatting issues, about 50 in total. Some sentences don't sound grammatical, some words don't make sense in context, and in a few cases, the language selection works correctly, but the formatting (dates, numbers, measurement units) doesn't match the expected locale. I've attached an Excel sheet with details. Let me know how we should track these. Should they be logged in Jira, or is there another process?"

I scrolled through the attached file. Some of the issues were familiar pain points in localization, that could slip through even the best automated processes. Others hinted at deeper structural problems in how we handled language and formatting.

I kept the email aside and quietly worked through my pending project brief, losing track of time for nearly half an hour, before turning to Nina, who was typing furiously at her keyboard.

"Coffee?" I asked.

She didn't even look up. “You know, when a Globalization Head invites me for coffee, it's never just about coffee. What's the catch?”

I grinned. “Fine. I need your localization wisdom. But I'm paying for the coffee.”

She sighed dramatically and pushed her chair back. “Alright, I'll take an overpriced latte in exchange for priceless knowledge.”

Fair trade.

The Core Discussion – Localization Over Coffee

The café was bustling, the aroma of freshly brewed coffee hanging in the air. Nina had already claimed a table by the window, stirring an absurd amount of sugar into her latte. I sat down across from her, my black coffee untouched.

“Did you see Arjan's email?” I asked, watching as she took a dramatic sip.

She smirked. “Oh, I saw it. Honestly, I was expecting it.”

That caught me off guard. “Expecting it? Why? We implemented localization properly, didn't we?”

She let out a chuckle. “Ah, the sweet optimism of a man who hasn't been burned by localization failures yet. Tell me, do you also think microwaves heat food evenly?”

I narrowed my eyes. “What's that got to do with anything?”

“Everything.” She perched on the edge of her seat, her eyes sharp. “Because just like a microwave, localization can look fine on the surface while secretly leaving cold spots everywhere. And if you're not careful, one day you bite into an ice-cold center of failure, like Arjan just did."

I sighed. "Alright, humor me. What are these 'cold spots'?"

Display Locales and Format Locales

She pulled out her phone and scrolled. "Let's start with the classics: display locale vs. format locale. You know how Arjan said his interface language was in English, but his dates and numbers weren't formatted correctly?"

I nodded. "Yeah, but isn't that a bug? Shouldn't everything follow the language setting?"

She let out a dramatic gasp. "No, no, no. That's exactly the kind of thinking that gets us localization folks stress migraines. Language and formatting are not the same thing! Say you move to Germany but still prefer your phone's UI in English. Does that mean you also want your dates in the American format?"

"I mean…" I hesitated.

She pointed at me like she just won a debate. "See. Some people want their display language in English, but their dates, numbers, and currency formatted according to their country's standards. That's why we separate display locale or UI language from format locale that determines how numbers, dates, and other units appear."

"Alright, fair point," I admitted. "But how did we miss this?"

She gave me a knowing look. "Because someone, no names mentioned, but let's call them 'everyone', thought one setting would cover it all."

I rubbed my forehead, considering. "So, what's the fix?"

"Two dropdowns instead of one. One for display locale, one for format locale. Let users decide how they want things to look. Otherwise, you get chaos. And you know what happens in chaos?"

"You get bug reports from Arjan?"

"Well… you bet." She clinked her coffee cup against mine.

This was going to be a long conversation.

Interpolation – The Art of Not Sounding Like a Robot

Nina stirred her coffee dramatically. "Alright, let's talk about one of the greatest crimes against localization: concatenation."

I took a sip of my coffee. "You know, I saw Arjan's email, and I get the grammar issues, but some of these errors… they feel so random. How can professional linguists make such grammatical mistakes? Isn't that literally their job? What are they doing? Playing word Jenga and hoping it doesn't collapse?"

She smirked. "Oh, absolutely. Right after they consult their Magic 8-Ball for translation advice." She tilted toward me, lowering her voice mock-seriously. "Look, linguists don't make grammar mistakes. They translate exactly what we give them. But if we give them sentence fragments, they'll translate them as they are. They don't know that our system plans to Frankenstein them together later."

I frowned. "So, they don't realize we're just smashing words together on our end?"

She took a triumphant sip of her coffee. “Bingo. They assume we know what we're doing.”

I winced. “Oof. Rookie mistake on their part.”

She grinned. “Oh, absolutely. They should know better than to trust developers.”

I laughed. “Okay, so if we don't want our system spitting out German sentences that sound like they were written by a malfunctioning chatbot, what do we do?”

She clapped. “Lesson one: Concatenation is evil. Instead of breaking sentences apart, we use placeholders. We send the whole sentence to translators: ‘The customer has {action} the order.' Then, in German, they can properly write: ‘Der Kunde hat die Bestellung {action}.'“

I nodded. “Okay, so it's not the linguists' fault. It's ours for not giving them the full picture.”

She grinned. “Ding ding ding! Give this man a prize.”

I chuckled. “Alright, no more concatenation. Got it. So, what's next on the list of ways we've unknowingly tortured languages?”

She propped an elbow on the backrest and smirked. “Pluralization. Because if you think ‘1 item' and ‘5 items' are easy in every language, you're in for a wild ride.”

Pluralization – When One Isn't the Loneliest Number

We had just finished discussing interpolation, and I was starting to feel like I was getting the hang of things. But Nina was not ready to let me off the hook just yet.

She took a sip of her coffee, wiped her lips with the back of her hand, and then grabbed a tissue from the napkin holder. She started folding it with unnecessary precision, as if preparing for some kind of dramatic demonstration.

“Alright, let's dive into pluralization,” Nina said with a grin, “And before you ask, yes, even in English, it's not as simple as it seems.”

Curious, I set my cup down. “Wait, what do you mean? English seems pretty straightforward for pluralization, right?”

She smiled wryly and raised an eyebrow, her fingers still working with the tissue. “Oh, my dear friend, never underestimate the complexity of English.” She pointed at me, “You might think ‘one apple, two apples' is the worst of it, but you'd be wrong. English is sneaky, and it likes to throw curveballs at you.”

I laughed. “I thought I was just dealing with one form: ‘apple' and ‘apples.' What else could there be?”

Nina inched closer, her eyes twinkling with mischief. “Well, consider this: You've got words like ‘child' and ‘children,' ‘mouse' and ‘mice.' That's not exactly straightforward, is it?”

The realization hit me. “Oh, right. I never thought of those.”

She smirked. “Exactly! Now, the worst part is when you start translating these sentences into other languages, because English doesn't have to deal with grammatical gender, complex plurals, or cases the way many other languages do.”

She paused dramatically, as though waiting for my brain to process the complexity. I nodded slowly, pretending to understand.

"So, what's the fix?" I asked.

Nina grabbed the tissue, unrolled it halfway, and began drawing an imaginary string with her finger. "In resource files, we need to structure our strings in a way that the system knows how to handle these different plural forms correctly. If we were to take a simple sentence like 'You have {count} messages,'" she said, "we would make sure that when the count is 'one,' it displays 'You have one message.' But if the count is any other number, we display 'You have {count} messages.' That's how we handle plurals."

She pointed to an imaginary string on the tissue and mimicked typing it out. "In English, it's not that bad. But some languages like Arabic, Russian, and Polish have multiple plural forms. And, trust me, we want to avoid sending the wrong plural form because the context can change entirely!"

I smiled, feeling a bit more confident. "Okay, so we just write a string that checks the number and chooses the right plural form?"

She nodded, clearly impressed by my progress. "Exactly! But here's the kicker. It's not just about picking a word based on the number; it's also about how you structure the string. You need to use the correct grammar to make sure it works in any language. And if you're not careful, that 'messages' can turn into a huge nightmare in other languages."

I took another sip of my coffee. "Sounds like we need a pretty flexible system."

I continued. "Okay, so we structure our strings carefully, we account for different plural forms, and we make sure things don't break when numbers change. That makes sense."

Gender Grammar: Respecting the rules

She smirked. “Good. Now imagine the same problem, but instead of just numbers changing words, what if the entire sentence structure had to change because of…” She paused, looking at me with an almost wicked grin.

I frowned. “Because of what?”

She tilted forward, lowering her voice as if revealing some grand mystery. “Because of gender.”

I frowned. “But our sentence structure doesn't change based on gender, right?”

Her eyes twinkled mischievously. “Oh, it absolutely does.”

I scoffed. “Come on. If I say, ‘He is a doctor' or ‘She is a doctor,' nothing else in the sentence changes except the pronoun.”

She picked up a napkin, tapping it against the table like a game show buzzer. “Ding ding ding! That's exactly the thinking that gets people into trouble with localization.”

I challenged. “Alright, prove me wrong.”

She grinned. “Gladly.”

She grabbed her tissue-paper-turned-whiteboard and scribbled something down. “Tell me, would you say, ‘He is a talented singer'?”

I nodded. “Obviously.”

She smirked. “And for a woman?”

“She is a talented singer.”

She pointed at me dramatically. "Bam! The verb didn't change, the noun didn't change; you're used to that consistency. But now let's try French: 'Il est un chanteur talentueux' for a man, but for a woman, it's 'Elle est une chanteuse talentueuse.' See the problem?"

I stared at the napkin. "...That's a lot of changes."

"And that's just one language." Nina's smile widened as she eased into the chair. "You should see what happens in Slavic languages. The whole sentence structure can change. One word tweak here, another shift there, suddenly it's unrecognizable."

I exhaled slowly. "So, if we're not handling gender properly, we're making our users cringe with bad grammar?"

She nodded. "Not just cringe. In some cases, the sentence might not even make sense. And remember, users don't blame the software. They blame us."

"Alright, so how do we fix this?" I wondered. "We can't possibly have separate strings for every gender, right? That would be a nightmare."

Nina grinned. "Bingo. That's why we use placeholders and rules." She grabbed the tissue paper again, sketching out an example.

"Imagine instead of hardcoding 'chanteur talentueux' or 'chanteuse talentueuse' directly in the resource file, we store two versions and pick the right one dynamically."

She scribbled something down:

```
talentedSinger.male = Il est un chanteur
talentueux.
```

```
talentedSinger.female = Elle est une
chanteuse talentueuse.
```

“Then, based on the user's profile or context, we pick the right version at runtime. That way, we're not messing around with string concatenation or weird inline replacements.”

I nodded, starting to see the pattern. “So, instead of hardcoding a generic ‘singer' and hoping the grammar stays intact, we let the system choose the right phrasing?”

“Exactly. And in languages where gender doesn't matter, we just have one version. But in languages where it does, we respect the rules.”

I frowned. “But what if we don't know the gender of the user? What if we need a neutral option?”

She tapped the tissue paper thoughtfully. “Some languages have a neutral form, but many don't. In those cases, we have to rework the sentence entirely to avoid gendered words. Instead of saying ‘He/She is a talented singer,' we might say ‘This person is talented at singing.'“

I exhaled. “Wow. So, localization isn't just translating words. It's sometimes rewriting entire sentences to fit the grammar.”

Nina laughed. “Welcome to my world.”

Repeat after me: Repetition isn’t bad

I unlocked my phone and slid a few inches across the table, still staring at the spreadsheet Arjan had sent. “I've seen some comments about translations,” I said, tapping the screen. “A lot of them were perfect in earlier versions, but now, some words have been translated incorrectly. What happened?"

Nina, who had been absentmindedly stirring her coffee, looked up with a knowing smile. "Ah, this is probably a case of regression, my friend."

"Regression? What do you mean?"

Nina took a sip of her coffee, then set her cup down with a soft clink. "Let me explain. It all really comes down to consistency. You've probably heard of the DRY principle in coding: Don't Repeat Yourself. The idea is to avoid duplicating things unnecessarily. But here's where it gets tricky when dealing with language."

"So, you mean we were trying to avoid duplication by reusing the word 'Open'?"

Nina nodded, then flicked her napkin open and smoothed it flat on the table. "That's what it looks like. We had just one instance of the word 'Open' in the resource file, and it was used for both the button and the status label. In English, everything looked fine, 'Open' on the button, 'Open' as a status. No problem. But then, when translators saw the word 'Open' used as a status, they assumed it was only being used in that context. So, they translated 'Open' as an adjective, thinking it was describing the status."

"So, the issue arose because of context?"

Nina gave a small chuckle. "Ah, that's where it gets tricky. The issue didn't arise for the status initially because it was correct in that context. 'Offen' as a status was fine. But when someone revisited the word 'Open' on the button, thinking that something was wrong, they corrected it to the verb form 'Öffnen.'"

I paused, processing this. “Wait, so when the translators fixed the word to work for the button as a verb, the status was fine, but the button became wrong?”

Nina nodded with a sigh. “That what happed. When we initially had 'Open' as a verb, the button showed up wrong in German as an adjective ‘Offen', which didn't make sense. But when we corrected it to work for the button as a verb, the status, which was correct before, started showing up wrong because the word was now incorrectly being treated as a verb. It's a classic case of one translation affecting the other.”

“Ah, I see. So, context really matters. The same word can't be reused for different meanings in different contexts without causing trouble.”

Nina smiled. “Right. DRY works great in code, but in translation, context is king. If we reuse words across different components or places, it can lead to all kinds of unintended issues. One change in context and everything falls apart.”

Nina leaned back in her chair, her expression shifting from a casual smile to something more thoughtful. “So, how do we avoid these kinds of issues in the future?”

I was eager to hear her thoughts. “That's what I was wondering.”

She tapped her fingers on the table, gathering her thoughts. “Well, the first step is simple: never, ever reuse the same string for different contexts. Even if it feels like it saves time or keeps things neat in code, it can cause translation chaos later on. We need to ensure that each context gets its own dedicated string.”

“So, you're saying we need to duplicate the string? That doesn't sound very DRY,” I said, using air quotes for effect.

Nina chuckled. “I know, I know. DRY is important in code. But when it comes to localization, sometimes you just have to let go of the ideal. Sure, duplication isn't great in theory, but it's far better than having confusing or incorrect translations. We can't treat every string like a one-size-fits-all.”

She paused, letting the weight of her words sink in. “Also, we need to make sure that when we do reuse a word or phrase, we provide the context. We could add comments or documentation to make sure that translators understand how a word is being used in a specific context.”

“Okay, so, if we had kept the button 'Open' as its own string and had added a separate one for the status ‘Open', we wouldn't have run into this?”

“Exactly,” Nina said, nodding. “And if we'd made sure the translator understood the button's context, we could have avoided the mix-up.”

“Right. So, it's about being explicit and not assuming context will be understood across the board,” I mused.

Nina smiled. “Yes. It's all about providing clarity. When in doubt, provide more context. If that means adding extra strings for different contexts, then that's what we need to do.”

I nodded, finally understanding the balance between the technical side and the linguistic side. “Got it. Make sure every context is clear, and don't assume the same word works everywhere.”

Nina gave a satisfied nod. “That's the spirit. Localization is as much about communication as it is about coding. The clearer we are, the better the results.”

As Nina finished her coffee, I couldn't help but feel a bit more clarity on how we could prevent future issues. The whole discussion on consistency, context, and gender-specific translations had me thinking about the broader implications for our localization strategy.

"So, Nina," I said, looking for a solution, "how do we put all this into some sort of system, something we can share with content writers, UX designers, and linguists? I want to make sure we're all on the same page, so we don't keep running into the same problems down the road."

Nina looked thoughtful for a moment, then grinned. "Alright, let's put this together into a set of guidelines, something simple but clear that we can share across teams. You know, like a 'Localization Bible'... without all the holy scrolls and incense."

I raised an eyebrow. "That sounds… very official. Go on."

Nina chuckled. "Alright, here's the plan. And don't worry. I'll keep it in plain English. No 'cathedrals of localization' here, I promise."

- - -

As I drove home, my mind wandered. The rhythmic hum of the tires on the road was almost meditative, but then a memory from the past suddenly popped into my head, making me smile to myself.

I remembered that one evening at home, when things had seemed peaceful until the all-too-familiar sound of my children's voices rose in the living room. I walked in to find Vihaan and Kashika in the middle of an intense argument.

Kashika, her arms crossed, looked like she was ready to win this one. “I told you, we're having a match later, and you said ‘okay',” she said firmly, glaring at Vihaan.

But Vihaan wasn't having it. With a mischievous smirk, he shot back, “No, no. You said we're having a match later, but I have already brought you the match. I thought you meant a match to light the candles!” He raised his eyebrows, clearly proud of himself.

Kashika groaned in frustration. “Ugh, you know I meant a game of Ludo! Not that kind of match!”

And then, to make it worse, Vihaan kept on pressing a box of matches on Kashika's shoulder with a grin. “Well, you said match, so I assumed this kind of match!”

I couldn't help but chuckle, standing at the doorway and watching the scene unfold. It was like a little battle of words, with each one using the ambiguity of homonyms to their advantage.

I rested my shoulder against the doorframe, smiling. “You two should really start a class on how to argue using homonyms. It's practically an art form by now.”

They both stopped, realizing how ridiculous it all was, leaving their little battle unresolved. Vihaan acted as if he had won the argument, and Kashika felt cheated.

As I drove home from the office, that moment replayed in my head. It was funny how something as simple as a match could cause so much chaos. I smiled to myself, thinking that homonyms, in all their multiple meanings, could really turn any innocent situation into a full-blown verbal sparring match. It was an unintended but entertaining weapon in their little arguments.

My Diary Notes

- **Don't hardcode text.** It makes translation harder and creates long-term issues.
- **Avoid reusing strings in different contexts.** What makes sense in one place may confuse in another.
- **Never concatenate translatable text.** Languages don't follow the same word order.
- **Plural rules vary by language.** Always support true pluralization logic.
- **Gender matters in many languages.** Ignoring it can break both grammar and user trust.
- **Display locale isn't enough.** Use content locale to show users what's truly relevant.
- **Context is everything.** Translators can't guess what a vague word like "open" really means.
- **Prepare before you translate.** Internationalization upfront saves huge rework later.
- **Strings carry meaning, not just words.** Treat them with care and clarity.
- **Testing in English alone isn't enough.** Other languages can break layouts or logic.
- **UI must be flexible.** What fits in English may overflow in other languages.
- **Translation is a process, not a step.** Keep improving with user feedback.

Chapter 8: Globalization QA

Scaling Trust

Terms you need to know	
Term	**Definition**
Visual Diff	(short for *Visual Difference*) A testing technique that compares visual snapshots (screenshots) of an application's UI before and after a change, to detect unintended changes in layout, style, or content.

Nov 16, 2023

A typical morning. Lukewarm coffee, Slack pings, Jira notifications. I had just minimized "Sprint Planning: Week 9" when my phone buzzed.

Lorenzo Santoro. Not someone who usually calls unless the ship's on fire.

I answered.

"Lorenzo?"

There was no "hello."

"Sourabh, I am setting up a meeting post lunch today. I need you in a meeting. We've got a situation with one of our top customers in Japan. Something made it to production that shouldn't have. A localization bug: on the executive dashboard, no less. Their CEO saw it live during a demo."

My pulse quickened.

"Wait… this was part of the last QA cycle, right?"

"That's what I thought, too. But clearly, something slipped. The bug itself isn't my worry; I know our talented team would fix it. I want to know why the bug leaked and what we can do to ensure it doesn't happen again.

Grab whoever you need. Find why this happened, and how we can prevent this from happening. I'll see you in the conference room at 2:00 PM."

The line went dead.

I sat frozen, staring at the phone and the laptop. The cursor was blinking on my half-written Confluence doc like it was mocking me. A major customer. A production issue. And the kind of email no one wants to get on a weekday morning.

We treat bugs as some embarrassing failure, a crack in our genius. But the truth is, they're not the enemy. They're part of the terrain.

The problem isn't that the bug occurred. The real failure is that it wasn't caught in time.

That's where our craft comes in. Not to create perfect systems, but to design a net fine enough to catch the imperfections before they fall into the hands of the user.

Just then, a knock at my door. Suhani Patel, our QA Manager, strode in, brisk, all business.

"Saw the incident report," she said, stepping inside and closing the door behind her without a word. "We've got a problem."

“Tell me,” I muttered, swiveling in my chair. “Lorenzo just called me. This one's bigger than just a bug. I need you on this, Suhani. Can you rally the QA team?”

She popped open her laptop, already scanning through tabs.

“I saw the incident report. We're doing QA through external vendors, but I have a feeling the test coverage wasn't aligned with our latest rollout. There's a chance our review cycles didn't match what hit prod.”

I stared at the ceiling for a second, letting it sink in. “Hmmm. I think we need to get to the bottom of this. Can you pull in your QA team for a quick meeting?”

“Already messaged them. Let's head to the war room.”

We walked briskly through the corridor, past the design pod and the engineering bay. As we entered the conference room. Ava was there with markers. Marco's pixelated Zoom tile appeared.

Time for answers.

Crisis Meeting Begins – Digging into the QA Leak

The room felt heavy with pressure, a mix of in-person and Zoom faces on the screen. Suhani sat beside me, already typing. Priya, Danylo, and Meiling from **Langutrix** (briefed by Suhani) joined us in person and on-screen, their focus sharp. I appreciated Suhani's experienced calm, but a knot remained in my stomach.

I usually hated fire-drill meetings. They smelled of chaos, and chaos didn't scale. But here we were.

I stood up to break the silence.

"Let's get right into it. We already know what went wrong. The executive dashboard broke in the Japanese locale. A localization bug made it to production, visible to the CEO of one of our top customers during a live demo."

The air shifted. Suhani leaned forward.

"I've pulled logs, test plans, and timelines," she said. "We'll get to the root cause, but first, we need to understand how this slipped through our QA process."

I nodded. "That's the first question: Why did this escape our QA process?"

Danylo, unmuted. "As a process, we do the linguistic testing of tier one languages that, over here, consists of English, German, French, Spanish, and Koren. We received the final build three days before the release. And hence performed testing in these languages."

Meiling jumped in. "We didn't have time for deep functional testing across all twelve locales. We ran quick UI smoke tests. We did our usual mix-and-match coverage: screens in one language, flows in another."

Suhani chimed in. "That's exactly the problem. Manual testing like this doesn't scale. We're officially supporting twelve locales, but realistically, we only had solid coverage on four or five. The rest were … 'best effort.'"

I could see nods around the room, and the weight of unspoken acknowledgment.

"And what about the current approach overall?" I asked. "Question two: *What's our current style of L10N and I18N QA?*"

Priya answered cautiously. “It's mostly manual. Click-throughs, visual checks for broken strings, layout issues, misalignments.”

Suhani added, “We don't consistently test locale-specific functionality: date and number formatting, plural rules, or right-to-left layouts are tested visually, but if they impact any functionality, we don't test. And accessibility? Not part of the current scope.”

The room was quiet for a beat too long.

“So essentially,” I said, “we've been validating translations by looking at them, but we haven't been *testing* them as part of the user experience.”

Exactly the gap we needed to close.

Only the projector fan filled the quiet, a dull mechanical breath. The whiteboard was already starting to fill with scribbled locales and release week timelines.

Suhani took a sip of her coffee and gently nudged the conversation forward.

Limitations of Manual Testing

“Alright, so we've agreed we lacked sufficient coverage. But let's talk about the elephant in the room…” She said, clicking the remote and highlighting the next point on the agenda.

“What are the risks of relying on our current approach - only manual testing?”

Rajiv, one of our senior QA engineers from Langutrix, adjusted his watch and spoke up. He had the calm tone of someone who'd seen more bugs than he cared to admit.

“Manual testers can only catch what they see, and that too, when they know what to look for,” he said. “Our team isn't fluent in all supported languages. Some testers might recognize visual glitches, but they won't always catch locale-specific formatting issues, or cultural nuances in copy.”

He paused and added thoughtfully, “You know how your nose is always visible to your eyes, but your brain learns to ignore it?”

A couple of us raised our eyebrows. I asked, “What's the connection?”

“It's called **perceptual adaptation**,” Rajiv explained. “We stare at the same UI every day. We stop noticing things: low contrast, misaligned elements, even untranslated strings. Our brains filter out what we *assume* is correct.”

Aisha chimed in. “That's true. It's even worse during regression. We're so focused on validating what's changed, we miss what broke elsewhere. Like the Brazilian Portuguese layout issue last time, nobody flagged it until it hit production.”

Suhani gave a slow nod, thoughtful. “And the stakes are higher than most people think. These bugs aren't just cosmetic. They affect usability, accessibility, and trust. A broken layout in Japanese isn't ‘just a visual bug' when the user can't complete a workflow.”

There was a moment of silence.

I broke it. “So, we're saying our current approach is reactive, not preventative. We rely on intuition and attention, which are both prone to human limits.”

Suhani moved the discussion forward. "Then let's not keep relying on what our brains filter out. What can we *automate* to support this effort?"

What can we automate to support this effort?

The question sharpened in my head. I turned to the whiteboard. "Let's say we want to move beyond reactive testing. How do we scale our QA efforts without losing coverage, especially across languages?"

Aisha jumped in. "We can start by automating locale switching and capturing UI snapshots in every supported language. Then use visual diffing tools to flag layout shifts, missing elements, or broken hierarchies."

"Absolutely," said Rajiv, adjusting his glasses. "But it shouldn't stop at visuals. Static code analysis can scan for hardcoded strings, missing translation keys, improper encodings…, even potential bidirectionality issues. These are easy to miss manually, especially in large codebases."

Suhani chimed in, "Pseudo-localization should be part of our dev pipeline. Stretch the text, flip directionality, inject special characters. If anything breaks, we'll know long before real content arrives."

"And we need unit tests," she added firmly. "Locale logic for currency, pluralization, number formatting, and date-time rules, these should be automated. There's no reason a regression should make it to production."

Aisha pointed to the projected dashboard. "People think automation is only about speed. But it's also about consistency. Machines don't get tired. They don't 'miss' things because they're familiar with the screen. They treat every locale as if they're seeing it for the first time."

Then she paused, frowning slightly. "But writing unit tests for every component? That's not sustainable. We'll burn out."

I let that sit. "Yeah... I hear you. So maybe the better question isn't *how much* to automate, but *what's worth automating...where it makes the most impact.* I don't know if you have heard this before, but we discussed taking an economic view while we were scoping for globalization. Now, we need scope for Globalization QA automation."

That opened the floodgates.
Rajiv adjusted the cuff of his sleeve, eyes narrowing slightly. "We need a tiered approach. Not everything needs the same level of scrutiny. Some logic is worth hammering with tests. Other stuff? Just needs a sanity check."
Aisha nodded. "For example, locale formatting, currencies, numbers, pluralization, that should live in shared utils. One function thoroughly tested. The components using it don't need to test formatting again. They're just rendering."
"Exactly my point," Rajiv said. "The real risk is in logic duplication. If every component rolls its own formatter, *that's* when bugs creep in."
Suhani capped the whiteboard marker with a soft snap and nodded to herself while drawing a pyramid on the whiteboard. "Okay, bottom layer: unit tests for locale logic. Middle layer: component tests, but only for rendering the right keys and surviving edge cases. Top layer: integration or E2E tests for things like locale switching, language persistence, and screen flows."
"Don't forget pseudo-locales," Aisha added. "That gives us layout stress tests without writing new test logic."
We stepped back, looking at Suhani's pyramid diagram. It was simple, but elegant.
"Not everything needs a spotlight. Just make sure the important things don't hide in the shadows."

There was a pause. Everyone seemed to be absorbing that.

"But automation has limits," I said slowly, turning back to the team. "A bot can tell you a button is misaligned, it can't tell you if the phrasing is off, or if a metaphor in Spanish feels awkward or even offensive. That takes cultural context. That takes human eyes."

Suhani nodded, "Agreed. We're not automating to replace ourselves. We're automating so that we can focus on the deeper, subtler stuff, so our time goes into things machines can't do."
I took a step back from the whiteboard. This didn't feel like another checklist conversation. We were thinking in layers, automation for breadth, humans for depth.

Can TDD be applied to i18n and l10n logic?

I pushed a thought further. "So, we've talked about automation for layout and visual bugs. But let's go deeper. Can we build localization logic right into our test strategy? Like a true TDD for i18n?"

Aisha didn't hesitate. "Great idea! That makes me think. For example, we could have a test that asserts the French locale always uses a space before the currency symbol. Or that unsupported locales gracefully fall back to English."

Rajiv chimed in. "And pluralization logic, too. In Russian, you've got different forms for one, few, and many. We could catch all that with automated unit tests."

I nodded. "Good. Because if we're writing business logic for pricing, date formatting, or grammar rules, and we don't have tests, then we're just 'hoping' it works."

Suhani glanced around. "We can even test things like accessibility. Are lang attributes set? Are screen reader texts changing with locale? It's not just about what's visible."

That's when Aisha raised an important point. "Right now, we only test contrast ratios and alt texts in English. We haven't really looked at how screen readers behave with Arabic or Hindi. Some of these scripts behave differently, and our QA team might not even be aware of those nuances."

Are we considering accessibility and inclusivity in our QA process?

"And there's another angle, language sensitivity," I added. "Some languages encode gender into every verb. Are we testing how our app handles that? Do we even have a glossary for inclusive language per locale?"

Suhani took a breath. "Honestly, we haven't gone that far. We're not yet validating culturally sensitive terms or checking if translations carry unintended bias. We're still treating localization like a string replacement task."

Rajiv added quietly, "And inclusivity is more than just translating text. It's making sure content is respectful, the experience is smooth, and users don't feel alienated."

There was a pause.

"Well," I said, "then let's start. We've got to raise the bar. Localization isn't a last-mile activity. It needs to be baked into how we test, how we automate, and how we think."

Suhani nodded. "Let's work on building that into our QA design. No more afterthoughts."

Setting Severity and Priorities of L10N/I18N bugs

Suhani tucked a stray lock of hair behind her ear and looked around the table. "Alright, team, let's shift gears. The way we've been labeling bugs, especially for localization, feels inconsistent. I think we need to revisit how we define Severity and Priority."

There were some nods around the room. I added, “Yeah, I've seen a few tickets where a typo in the footer was marked as 'High Severity'. Meanwhile, a broken Arabic layout that blocked a critical action had a ‘Medium' tag.”

Suhani sighed. “Exactly my point. If we want to get better at triaging, we need to speak the same language. So, let's walk through this together.”

I jumped in. “Severity is all about the impact of the bug on the system. If it breaks functionality, causes data loss, or makes the app unusable, that's high or critical severity.”

“And it's usually QA or developers who set severity,” Aisha said, catching on. “We're the ones seeing the technical fallout.”

Suhani nodded. “Correct. Priority, on the other hand, is about urgency. It's a business decision. How soon does this need fixing, and why? There could be many reasons, the cost of delay, the alignment with a certain event, or maybe, a key customer needs something to be fixed before other issues. That's where PMs or delivery leads step in.”

I tapped an imaginary scale midair with two fingers. “Let's think of it like this, Severity is about the damage the bug causes. Priority is about how quickly we need to act.”

“So,” Aisha asked, “would a login page failure always be high severity?”

“Pretty much,” I said. “A valid login throwing an error? That's blocking access, definitely high severity. But if it only affects a small group, say internal admins using a legacy browser, the priority might be low. We'd still fix it, just not right away.”

Suhani followed up. “Now, take a misaligned icon on the dashboard. It's a visual flaw, low severity. But if our top

Japanese client points it out during a demo? That instantly becomes a high priority because of visibility."

We all chuckled, slightly sheepish.

Suhani, noticing the laughter, thought of bringing seriousness to her statement. "I meant, after all it's a customer reported issue and hence a higher priority."

Aisha tapped her stylus against the table. "Okay, how about a real-time example: Arabic layout breaks on invoice preview. It doesn't crash anything, but fields overlap."

"That's High Severity," I said. "It affects usability and it's in production."

"But maybe only Medium Priority if no customer has complained yet," Suhani added. "Unless a sales meeting comes up in the Middle East. Then it spikes."

"Got it," Aisha said, typing fast. "So, the same bug can carry different combinations depending on both the impact and the urgency."

"Right," I smiled. "And that's why we need a shared understanding, not just drop-downs in Jira."

Aisha spun her laptop around. "I've been taking notes. How about something like this?"

Severity	Priority	Example
Critical – System crash, data loss/corruption, app not usable	**Fix immediately** (ASAP)	App won't load; users stuck on splash screen
High – Major feature broken; some workaround may exist	**Fix in next release**	Invoice not downloadable in Arabic locale
Medium – Minor issue, not blocking	**Fix after high-priority bugs**	Label truncation settings
Low – Cosmetic issue	**Fix if time permits**	Tooltip misaligned on mobile screen

Suhani gave a satisfied nod. “This works. Let's clean it up and make sure everyone is aligned.”

“And maybe we can color-code this into our ticket templates,” I added.

Aisha smiled as she closed her laptop. “This already feels more grounded. Like we're not just debating labels anymore.”

Suhani's posture softened, finally relaxing a little. “That is what we are trying. Don't think of it as red tape, but having a predictable process.”

There was a pause, just long enough to breathe, before Suhani said, “So what do we want this to look like moving forward? Not just for this bug, but for everything that comes after?”

Aisha cut in, voice quick, like she'd been waiting to say it, “Here's a combo that can scale.”

She started listing, ticking them off on her fingers:

“Linguistic testing by native speakers.”

“Pseudo-localization, built into early dev stages. Catch layout issues before we even involve translators.”

“Unit and integration tests for anything locale-sensitive like currency, date formats, plural rules…”

“Visual regression testing. Snapshot the UI in different locales and catch layout breaks automatically.”

“Also, we need automation that flags hardcoded strings and untranslated keys. No excuses there.”

“And accessibility audits. In *every* supported language. Not just English. Alt text, screen reader support, keyboard navigation, among others.”

“Functional smoke tests. Run them across all locales, every regression cycle. Even if it's just a high-level sanity check.”

Someone added, “Let's also throw in automated tests for date/time formatting, string fallbacks, number precision…”

“And accessibility,” Suhani said firmly. “That one's not optional. Not anymore.”

There were no more objections, just quiet agreement. Everyone could feel it.

As the ideas settled into something more structured, someone, probably Neeraj, began jotting them down on the whiteboard. Not bullet points, but groupings. Clusters of what could happen *now*, what could wait a few weeks, and what might evolve into long-term practice.

Suhani nodded, reading aloud from the scribbles. "Alright, here's where we are. This isn't the final word, but it's something we can shape over the next few days."

Immediate Actions

"We'll start with a bug severity and priority matrix. Not just for engineering, but one that everyone, including PMs and QA, can use with clarity."

"Second, let's identify automation tools for visual diffs, and linting tools to flag hardcoded or missing translation keys."

"We also need to implement pseudo-localization in our pipeline, early, maybe even before strings go to translation."

Mid-term Plan

"Let's bring localization checks into our CI/CD, so every commit is at least checked for obvious i18n issues."

"Add regression testing across locales. Not full coverage in every sprint, but enough to catch common layout or truncation problems."

"And we need to help our linguists, too. Style guides, terminology glossaries, it'll make everything more consistent."

Long-term Vision

Suhani rolled the marker between her fingers, thinking. "Eventually, this isn't just about bugs, it's about the experience."

"A unified global QA strategy. One that covers localization, internationalization, accessibility, and inclusivity. All of it."

Nobody objected.

It was surely a direction, not a plan written in stone. And sometimes, that's all a team needs to start moving together.

The discussion eventually began to slow. People leaned back, tapped shut their laptops, or glanced at their phones, but not with disengagement, more with a shared mental fatigue. We had covered a lot. And for a meeting that had been thrown together on the fly, it felt surprisingly cohesive.

Suhani was jotting down action items on her notepad, a faint smile returning to her face for the first time that day.

Later, the whiteboard fading in my memory, I briefed Lorenzo on the root cause and our agreed resolution, and how it could be a foundational shift.

He listened quietly, nodding – a shared understanding of overdue change, no drama needed.

- - -

That night, after the long day, I came back home to the comforting scent of caramelizing sugar.

Ritu was in the kitchen, completely absorbed in making a batch of her famous "Butter toffee". The counter was a quiet chaos:

measuring spoons, sticks of butter, a candy thermometer clipped to the side of the pan, and a bowl of toasted nuts ready for the final mix-in.

I crossed my ankles loosely and stayed by the door, just watching her work with the calm focus of someone who has done this enough times to trust both her senses and her tools.

She handed me a small spoon with a glossy ribbon of golden syrup. I tasted it, warm, nutty, sweet, just shy of caramelized.

She checked the thermometer and gave a small nod, stirring gently. “Almost there.”

That's when something clicked for me.

The thermometer didn't lie. The tools were exact. But even with all of that, the final judgment still came from her. From tasting, sensing, adjusting. That blend of instinct and precision is what made the result perfect.

It wasn't hard to see the parallel.

In QA, tools gave us scale, consistency, and speed. It was our thermometer, our measuring spoon. But the final layer, the feel of a UI, whether a string carries the right tone, or if the layout respects its cultural flow, those things demand human sensitivity.

Language has nuances that go far beyond correctness. A sentence might be grammatically accurate, yet completely off in tone or impact. A button label might fit, but feel awkward to a native speaker. No automated test could truly capture that. It needed intuition.

The problem wasn't automation or manual testing. It was when we forgot that they were meant to complement each other, not substitute one for the other.

As Ritu poured the bubbling toffee onto the tray and tapped it gently to even out, I made a quiet note to myself:

Never rely on a thermometer to tell you how something tastes.

- - -

That weekend, I briefed Naren via Zoom about the intense week – awkward questions, tough talks, and our evolving QA strategy. He listened patiently, nodding as usual. When I finished, there was a brief pause. He exhaled slowly and then said, “Every product has bugs. The difference is whether you find them… or your users do.”

I couldn't help but smile. It was simple. Obvious, even. But exactly what I needed to hear.

My Diary Notes

- **A bug seen by a customer is a bug seen by the world**: Visibility magnifies impact, prevention must begin before exposure.
- **A bug is not betrayal, it's a blind spot**: The fault lies not in its birth, but in our failure to catch it before it grows.
- **The nose is always there, but the eyes forget**: Familiarity breeds blindness. Only fresh eyes or tools can spot what's become invisible.
- **Automation is the thermometer; instinct is the taste**: Tools tell you "How hot," but only people know "how right."
- **Test cases can spot the bug, but only people feel the flaw**: Language and culture don't break, they disappoint.
- **Severity is impact. Priority is urgency.**
- Inclusivity is a mindset, not a feature.
- **A feature untested is a bug undiscovered**: Every bug is a customer lost in silence.
- Regression across locales is your early warning, not an afterthought.
- **The best QA strategy is a team of tongs and tongues.** Tools and technology scale, humans bring the soul.

Chapter 9: The Localization Operations

Where Linguistics meet Logistics

Terms you need to know

Terms	Definitions
Locale Data Steward	Role responsible for managing and maintaining locale data accuracy across teams and systems.
Systems of record	Authoritative systems where official data, like locale info, is stored and maintained.
Master source of truth	A single, reliable source for consistent locale data across platforms.
Kanban	A visual workflow management method that helps teams limit work in progress and improve efficiency by visualizing tasks on a board.
LangOps orchestrator	A central system that automates and manages localization workflows across product and marketing teams.
DevOps	Combined development and operations practices that enable fast, automated software delivery.
TMS (Translation Management System)	A platform that manages and automates the translation process, often via API integrations.
Linguistic assets	Core language resources like translation memories, glossaries, and style guides.
TMs (Translation Memories)	Databases that store past translations for reuse and consistency.
XLIFF files	Standard XML-based files used to exchange translatable content between systems and translators.
Middleware	Software that connects systems to enable data exchange and process automation.
Webhooks	Real-time triggers that send data between systems when events occur.
Event-driven hooks	Actions automatically triggered by specific system events, such as data changes.
Watchers	Scripts or tools that monitor systems and run scheduled imports when changes are detected.

Terms you need to know	
Terms	**Definitions**
Locale metadata tagging	Adding language and region info to data for analytics and tracking.

Feb 12, 2024

The first hint that something big was brewing came not through Slack, nor an executive memo, but in the way people began tidying up their documentation. Confluence pages, once left to decay, were suddenly resurrected. Old diagrams were retouched. CI/CD dashboards got a cosmetic scrub. Even the snack area received fresh stock, as if clean granola bars could signal operational maturity.

Word spread quickly: *LinguaLogic Partners* was coming.

And not just anyone. Diana Preston and Reed MacAllister.

Their names carried weight. Diana's LocOps checklists had quietly become the backbone of many enterprise workflows, while Reed's internal playbooks circulated across teams like treasured contraband: annotated, adapted, and rarely credited. People in our world generally don't get famous. These two were the exceptions.

It was Naren who had suggested that I get our current LocOps reviewed by external experts, an unbiased reality check on how we managed end-to-end localization in Comventra's fast-scaling ecosystem. Upon my request, leadership had brought them in to conduct a three-day LocOps audit. Luckily they were a part of our existing consulting vendor, *LinguaLogic Partners*. I was told, with vague authority, that I'd be "shadowing" them. Translation: follow them around, give context when asked, and above all, don't get in the way.

The Arrival

They arrived precisely at 8:55 a.m., not early enough to look overeager, not late enough to signal disorganization. Diana walked in first, carrying a slim laptop bag and a thin paper notebook, the one with a Moleskine cover and immaculate handwriting within. She greeted the front desk by name. How? No one knew. Reed followed moments later, juggling a stylus, a foldable keyboard, and two phones, one of which chirped every time a calendar event changed time zones.

They introduced themselves like seasoned consultants: warm, polite, efficient.

"Diana Preston," she said, shaking my hand firmly. "Audit lead. And you must be Sourabh. I've read some of your string management notes from the S3 pipeline docs. Smart thinking on fallback policies."

Well… someone noticed. That doc had six views. One of them had been Diana.

Reed gave a nod, already scanning the TV monitor in the hallway that looped our product demo. "Looks like you've already wired in CI blockers for unwrapped strings. That's solid. Visual diffs too?"

I nodded. "We run snapshots and layout tests across major locales. RTL as well."

"Nice," he said, genuinely impressed. "Not many folks get that far. Curious though, do you have rollback hooks tied to feature flags when localized deployments fail?"

I hesitated. "We have partial coverage. It's not unified across environments yet."

He tapped his pen against the table, already sketching a box labeled `Rollback Orchestrator`.
"Got it. We'll dig into that tomorrow."

The Kickoff Room

The kickoff took place in Glasshouse, our conference room, recently outfitted with fresh markers, multiple HDMI dongles, and a spread of croissants that no one would touch after Diana politely declined one.

Amira arrived early, laptop open, tabs arranged like chess pieces. Nina and Marco followed, flanked by Ava and Suhani, each carrying notepads and questions dressed as updates. I could feel the collective breath-holding as Diana clicked open her first slide.

Title: "Globalization Audit Kickoff – Comventra LocOps"

Diana clicked to the next slide and took a small step forward, "Let's keep it simple," she said. "LocOps, or Localization Operations, is how localization actually runs in real life, not just in theory."

"It's the set of tools, workflows, automations, and decisions that make localization happen *on time, at scale, and without surprises.* It's what connects your product teams, language teams, and release pipelines into one working system."

She paused to let that land, "If localization is *what* we deliver, LocOps is *how* we deliver it again and again, reliably, across languages and platforms."

Diana looked up, eyes scanning each person before she continued, "What makes or breaks global scale isn't the number of languages. It's the machinery behind them. The choreography of systems, people, and decisions that make localization feel *invisible* to the user and *predictable* to the org."

"Why does it matter?" she asked, then answered herself. "Because *scale* demands repeatability. And *quality* demands clarity."

Diana clicked forward again. The next slide read:

Core Pillars of LocOps

Automation. Integration. Scalability. Observability.

She turned to the room with a half-smile, "Buzzwords, right? Let's break them down. No jargon."

She pointed to the first word.

1. Automation

"This means getting rid of manual steps. When a developer finishes a feature, localization tasks should trigger automatically. No tickets, no waiting. Same with delivering translations back. Less copy-paste, more click-and-go."

Marco raised a hand slightly, tapping his pen, "We do that in dev branches. But fallback to manual happens in hotfixes." Reed made a note, "Interesting. Let's look at that edge case later today."

2. Integration with DevOps

"Your localization flow should live where your development lives in CI/CD, in source control, in your release tools. If your code is ready but your strings are stuck in a spreadsheet, you're not integrated."

Amira nodded, "We've wired in triggers post-merge, but we still hit friction with context handoff to linguists."
Diana looked intrigued. "Good. Let's trace that context flow. Those are the pain points that scale breaks."

3. Scalability

"What works for 2 languages might break with 20. LocOps needs to scale more content, more locales, more teams, without creating chaos. That means smart workflows and systems that don't choke when things grow."

Ava interjected gently, "We're getting bottlenecks at five locales already, mostly on review cycles."
Reed flipped to a fresh tab on his tablet, "Noted. Let's chart that out."

4. Observability

"You can't fix what you can't see. You need dashboards, logs, alerts. Know what's translated, what's pending, what failed. Not just for translators, for PMs, engineers, QA. Everyone should see the same map."

Suhani leaned forward, "We've been piloting a loc-status overlay on our QA portal. It's helping, but it's fragile."
Diana smiled, "Great initiative. Fragility means opportunity.

She stepped back from the screen, "When localization breaks, it's rarely the words; it's the workflow. These pillars keep that workflow honest."

The room was calm and focused. Audit anxiety had given way to curiosity and the rare energy that comes when work feels valued. Questions shifted from tasks to systems.

“We're not here to nitpick,” Diana continued, “We're here to understand how your localization operations support your product scale. Our goal is not just to point out gaps. It's to trace opportunities.”

And just like that, the audit was expected to be carried out, not with judgment, but with curiosity.

Or at least, that's what we told ourselves.

Automation: The Silent Workhorse

We reconvened in the Glasshouse after a short coffee break. Diana placed her notebook down like a chessboard, ready to be played.

“Let's begin with **Automation**,” she said. “We'll move system by system. Sourabh, you'll provide context. And for implementation details, we'd like to hear directly from your leads.”

I motioned to Marco Rossi, already seated near the end of the table. Marco, our lead developer and the beating heart of our i18n automation, adjusted his hoodie and powered up his terminal.

Diana smiled, warm but precise. “Marco, walk us through your current **automated flow** from content creation to translated deliverables. Where does automation start, and where does it… hesitate?”

Marco cleared his throat.
"Sure. So, for product UI, we have an automated trigger tied to our Git repository. When devs merge code to the 'main' branch, an i18n linter runs, checks for hardcoded strings, missing resource keys, and encoding anomalies. If the commit passes, it pushes updated resource files to our TMS via API integration. Translations are requested automatically for supported locales."

He tapped a few keys. A clean Jenkins pipeline visual appeared on screen, "Once translations return from the TMS, the system automatically merges them into the localized branches. These are built in our CI/CD pipeline, and pseudolocalization tests are run on staging environments."

Reed's eyes sharpened. "Impressive. And for your marketing content, support docs, knowledge base?"

Marco shot me a glance. I took that one.

"Less streamlined," I admitted. "Marketing uses a separate CMS, Contentlify. There's no direct integration to the TMS. So, Ava's team manually exports XLIFF files, uploads them, then reimports the translations. Same goes for support articles."

Diana didn't frown. But she didn't nod either. She scribbled something in her notebook.

"And for rollback or error handling?" Reed asked. "Say a translation is incorrect, incomplete, or corrupt. How automated is your rollback?"

Marco winced slightly.
"Rollback for UI is semi-manual. We have locale fallback logic in code, but reverting translations in the TMS is still a human task. No automatic rollback triggers there."

Diana set her pen down softly.

"Okay," she said, her voice even. "Let's summarize:"

Automation Strengths	Automation Gaps
i18n linting on merge	Marketing/support CMS not integrated
API-based push/pull for UI	Manual XLIFF handling
Pseudolocalization tests auto-run	No automated rollback
	Vendor handoff semi-manual

"And here are some recommendations." She flipped to a fresh page and wrote:

Recommendations:

1. **Connect CMS to TMS**
   "Use available connectors or middleware (e.g., webhooks, API scripts) to automate content exchange."

2. **Automate Rollback**
   " Build pre-approved TM snapshots; implement locale-level revert triggers."

3. **Centralized Workflow Orchestration**
   "Consider a LangOps orchestrator that spans both product and marketing ecosystems."

Reed looked up. "Our view? You've nailed **product localization automation**. But **content ecosystem automation** is fragmented. Bridging that gap will halve your cycle times and reduce operational friction."

Marco nodded slowly, already thinking in diagrams.

By the end of Day 1, no conclusions were declared. Just quiet notes taken and gaps gently surfaced. The mirror had tilted; tomorrow, we'd see more clearly.

Day 2 - Integration

Glasshouse had settled into a quiet rhythm. Charts from yesterday's automation discussions still lingered faintly on the whiteboard corners.

Today, Amira began with measured confidence, "On the systems side, we've put solid foundations in place. Our localization environment integrates cleanly with our CMS and source control. We also maintain locale-specific product catalogs and country configurations tied to user accounts. This ensures users see the right languages, currencies, and formats."

She glanced at Diana, who gave an encouraging nod. "And how is that locale data maintained across your systems of record?"

Amira answered smoothly, "We synchronize locale tables between the user account database and the product catalog nightly. Regional settings propagate through those two main sources."

Reed rested his forearms on the table, his expression open yet analytical, "Two main sources. And what about your marketing site and help center? Do those consume locale configurations from the same systems?"

Amira answered, "Not directly. Marketing has its own CMS with a separate country selector. It's configured manually. Support content is based on Zendy, sorry, our help platform's settings, which also has a separate locale management."

Diana's pen hovered over her notebook. "So if a country's locale setting changes, say, new currency rules or legal disclaimers, how many systems require manual updates?"

Amira exhaled slowly, "At least four, counting mobile app config files."

Reed's voice stayed gentle, "And how do you ensure consistency across them? Any automated propagation?"

"No, it's coordinated manually via release notes and cross-team meetings."

Diana tapped her notebook thoughtfully, "And your analytics stack. Does it capture locale-specific usage cleanly? Do product event logs include locale metadata to guide localization priorities?"

Amira frowned. "Our analytics team collects region and language separately, but I don't believe those are tied directly to localization event tracking."

Reed nodded slowly, "Meaning if, say, Spanish users encounter higher drop-off in checkout, that insight won't feed directly into prioritizing localization improvements in that flow?"

"Not systematically, no."

Diana's gaze was steady but kind. "I see. And finally, feedback loops. How does customer support pass locale-specific issues back to your globalization team?"

Amira gave a wry smile, "They tag tickets by language manually, and we get an occasional summary report. But it's informal."

Reed flipped his notebook closed softly, "So… across systems… locale data exists in multiple places. But there's no **master source of truth**, nor an **automated flow** to keep those systems synchronized in real time."

Amira nodded slowly, realization dawning, "Our integration is strong within *isolated systems*. Cross-system data flows are fragile."

Diana smiled gently, "A common maturity inflection point. Integration isn't just about files and content. It's about **data cohesion** across the ecosystem."

For a few quiet seconds, only the soft scratch of writing filled the room.

When she finished, she pushed the notebook aside and glanced up, her gaze calm but direct. "Here's what I'm hearing," she said, tapping the notebook with her finger, "These are the **systemic gaps** we've uncovered in your integration fabric so far."

She read them aloud, her voice crisp:

1. **No centralized locale/country master data**
2. **Manual propagation of locale configurations across multiple systems**

3. **Lack of automated sync between product, marketing, support, and mobile platforms**
4. **Analytics and localization feedback loops, disjointed or incomplete**
5. **Risk of inconsistent user experience due to data fragmentation**

Amira sat back. The silence in the room was reflective, almost heavy with realization.

Diana closed her notebook gently and rested her hands on the table.
Her tone softened, slipping into that practiced cadence of a seasoned consultant easing a team from diagnosis to solution, "Amira, what you've built is a strong foundation. But as you scale, fractures in **data cohesion** don't stay minor. They compound. You'll need a strategy that ensures **systems think in unison** about locale and region data, rather than relying on human coordination."

Reed pressed his hands to the table, voice measured but precise, "Here's what we'd suggest as a roadmap. It doesn't need to be done all at once. But these layers will future-proof you."

He flipped to a fresh page and began sketching a loose diagram as he spoke.

1. Establish a Master Locale Service (MLS)

"First, centralize all locale-relevant data: languages, regions, currency formats, date/address schemas, compliance variants, into a single master data service."

Diana glanced at Reed, then added with a small nod, *"We can call it the Master Locale Service...MLS, for short. It becomes your source of truth."*

All downstream systems: product catalog, CMS, support, mobile apps consume this data via APIs or config pulls.

2. API-driven Sync Across Systems

Reed tapped his diagram, "Where possible, avoid batch/manual updates. Instead, expose **event-driven hooks** or scheduled **API syncs** to propagate changes from MLS to other platforms. For systems that can't consume APIs directly, build **watchers** or **scheduled import scripts**."

Amira nodded slowly, already mentally cataloging which systems could adapt easily.

3. Metadata Enrichment in Analytics & Feedback

Diana gestured thoughtfully, "Integrate **locale metadata tagging** into your analytics events and support ticketing flows. If you capture a locale at a point of interaction, you'll **close the feedback loop** between user behavior and localization needs."

Reed chimed in, "For example, if a checkout flow sees disproportionate drop-off in Germany, your MLS could flag that the payment terms or legal disclaimers are outdated there."

4. Governance and Ownership

Diana's gaze held Amira's firmly, but kindly, "None of this sustains without **clear ownership**.
We recommend defining a **Locale Data Steward** role, perhaps under your globalization team, who maintains MLS accuracy and coordinates with IT, marketing, and product teams."

Amira gave a slow, appreciative nod. Her earlier confidence hadn't eroded. It had sharpened.
She saw a path now, not just problems.

"I like it," she said simply. "We can work with this."

Reed grinned. "That's what we like to hear."

Afternoon Session: The Scalability Deep Dive

The sun had shifted by the time we regrouped in the room. The glass walls cast long rectangles of light across the table.
Marco had quietly left after the Integration session, and now it was Nina's turn.

Nina, our Localization Specialist, slid into the chair across from Diana and Reed with her usual quiet confidence. Her laptop was neatly stickered with flag icons and Unicode jokes. She was the keeper of our **linguistic assets**, and no one knew our translation memories better.

Diana greeted her warmly, "Nina, good to see you. Sourabh mentioned you've been leading the charge on localization quality and consistency."

Nina gave a modest nod, "Yes, I manage our TMs, glossaries, style guides, and coordinate handoffs with our external linguists."

Diana smiled. "Perfect. Today, we're zooming out a little to loo, how resilient are your processes and assets when volume or markets increase?"

Reed sat up a little straighter. “Maybe start by walking us through how things operate now, and where you feel confident, they'd scale.”

Nina clicked open a clean slide deck, “We maintain a centralized TM and glossary per language pair. They're versioned monthly, and translators access them via our TMS. We've standardized style guides in English and had them adapted for French, German, and Japanese, our top markets.”

She flipped to the next slide, “As for workflow scale: Right now, most requests, whether feature launches, campaign pushes, or support content, come through our localization request form, which Ava triages. I prep the linguistic assets, coordinate handoffs with translators, then manage QA and LQA.”

She looked up, satisfied, “We're confident this process works as we grow within our current markets.”

Diana nodded slowly, jotting a few notes. Then she asked, “Let's imagine ShopSphere adds four new markets in the next year: Brazilian Portuguese, Korean, Arabic, and Hindi. Walk me through how your current linguistic asset management and workflows would adapt.”

Nina hesitated, just a beat, “Well, we'd create new TMs and glossaries for each language pair, adapt style guides... and translators would get access through the same platform.”

Reed's voice was gentle but pointed, “How much overhead would that add to your monthly TM/versioning process? Do you foresee conflicts or duplication risks?”

Nina's brows furrowed slightly, “I suppose... quite a bit. Especially since our current TM update process is manual and localized per language. And the glossaries are maintained as spreadsheets for some markets. It could get messy fast."

Diana tucked a loose strand of hair behind her ear and jotted a few notes, "And if two regional product teams start launching features **at different cadences**, say, Germany wants feature X before Japan. How would you manage **locale-specific branching** of TMs, strings, and context notes?"

Nina exhaled slowly, "We don't have a branching model yet. Currently, it's one master TM per language, updated sequentially. Version conflicts... would be likely."

She sat back; lips pressed thinly. "I see the fault lines."

Diana nodded, writing neatly:

1. **TM/Glossary Management overhead balloons as locales increase**
2. **Manual versioning risks duplication and conflicts**
3. **Lack of locale-specific branching or differential releases**
4. **Workflow throughput bottlenecks (triage, QA) with rising request volume**
5. **Vendor capacity & scalability, unknown for sudden market expansion**

She slid the notebook slightly forward again, her trademark mirror move, "These are typical scale stress points. Let's walk through **how to reinforce them** before you get there."

Recommendations for Scalability

1. Modularize Linguistic Assets

Reed spoke first. “Break large, monolithic TMs into **modular, domain-specific segments**: UI strings, legal, marketing, support. That way, when markets expand, you can **reuse relevant modules**, not duplicate entire TMs.”

2. Implement TM Branching & Versioning

Diana added smoothly, “Introduce a **branching model** for TMs and glossaries that mirrors your product release branches. For example, ‘DE-feature-X branch', ‘JP-core branch'. Use delta updates and controlled merges rather than full overwrites.”

3. Automate Asset Sync & QA Workflows

Reed gestured to Nina, “Where possible, script **automated TM/glossary syncs**, especially across language pairs. And automate LQA task creation when asset versions update, reducing manual prep burden.”

4. Stress-test Vendor Capacity

Diana's tone sharpened slightly, “Run **vendor scalability tests** before expansion. Simulate a spike of 5x project volume and see how vendors respond in turnaround, quality, and communication.”

5. Re-architect Workflow Ownership

Reed concluded, “Don't over-centralize. As you scale, **decentralize triage and asset prep** by empowering regional leads or language leads. You'll reduce bottlenecks and distribute load."

Nina, to her credit, didn't bristle. Her brow furrowed, but it was the furrow of someone recalculating with purpose, "Alright," she said, pen already moving, "We can start modularizing the TMs this quarter. Branching... I'll work with Marco on feasibility."

Reed smiled approvingly, "That's exactly the mindset that scales."

- - -

As we packed up, Diana gave a small nod of satisfaction, "Integration makes the system coherent. Scalability makes it resilient."

We all left with full notebooks and a healthy sense of ambition for what was next.

Day 3 - Morning Session: The Power of Observability

By the third morning, something about the office felt sharper. There's a rhythm that sets in after two full days of deep audits. People start pre-emptively gathering artifacts, anticipating questions before they're asked.

I arrived early, nursing a second coffee. Diana and Reed were already there, seated at the long glass table, their notebooks stacked with geometric precision.

Diana glanced up with a small smile.
"Morning, Sourabh. How's your brain holding up?"

I grinned. “Warmed up and ready.”

She closed her notebook gently, “Today, we pivot to the fourth pillar: **Observability**. It's where all our previous discussions: automation, integration, scalability either stay coherent… or collapse under complexity.”

Reed glanced around, steepling his fingers, “Without visibility, scale and speed amplify **blind spots**. We don't want **more localized products** with **less understanding of what's actually happening**.”

Diana turned to me, “For this session, we'd like Suhani to join us, right?”

I nodded. Suhani had been patiently following the audit trail from afar, chiming in on Slack threads but letting others take center stage. Now it was her moment.

Moments later, she entered briskly, balancing her laptop and a blue notebook. Suhani was meticulous. Her QA dashboards were legendary for their precision.
She greeted us all with a nod and took her seat.

Diana folded her hands neatly. “Suhani, you've been overseeing localization quality assurance and reporting for a while now.
Walk us through the current landscape of **visibility and observability**. What you track, where stakeholders get insights, and where you feel confident.”

Suhani gave a short nod.

“Our observability focus currently splits into two areas: **Status dashboards** and **QA reporting**.

1. For **translation status**, we maintain a Kanban-style board that tracks requests at the macro level per language, per content type (UI, support, marketing). It's updated twice a week manually.

2. For **LQA,** or Localization Quality Assurance as we calle it, we log issues in spreadsheets categorized by error types: Mistranslations, functional defects, cultural issues, etc.
   We generate monthly reports summarizing quality by language and vendor.

3. For **release QA**, we track defect rates per sprint, including internationalization bugs and localization regressions. Those are visible in our main defect tracker."

She rested her chin lightly on her knuckles, thoughtful, "I believe stakeholders have decent visibility, especially on high-level status and defect trends."

Diana gave a soft hum, jotting brief notes. Then she tilted her head slightly, "Let's double-click on context visibility. How easily can a translator, or even an LQA tester, see where and how a string is used in the product? Do they get contextual metadata, screenshots, usage notes?"

Suhani's lips pressed briefly, "For translators, we add comments to strings where we anticipate ambiguity. For LQA testers, we share screenshots or staging links as needed. But it's ad hoc."

Reed's brow arched slightly. "Do translators ever report contextual mismatches? Strings that didn't make sense until they saw them live?"

Suhani exhaled, "Yes. We get those post-release occasionally. Especially in languages with gendered forms like German and French, where context shifts meaning."

Reed scribbled quickly.

Diana's next question came gently but firmly, "Now on operational observability, how easily can you, or leadership, see where localization bottlenecks or delays happen? For example, whether delays stem from engineering handoffs, translation backlog, QA rework, or vendor turnaround?"

Suhani hesitated a moment longer this time, "We can infer some of that based on timestamps in tickets and handoff dates… but there's no live end-to-end view of localization throughput. We rely on post-mortems if a launch slips."

Reed exhaled slowly and shifted in his chair. "And do stakeholders, say, PMs or Engineering, have self-service visibility into localization status on their features?"

Suhani shook her head slightly, "They ask Ava or me for updates. It's still very push-driven, not self-serve."

Diana flipped to a fresh notebook page, her brow furrowing slightly in focus. The room settled into that now-familiar quiet as she wrote crisply:

1. Limited in-context visibility for translators and testers
2. Ad hoc, manual annotation of string metadata
3. No real-time, end-to-end localization pipeline visibility
4. Manual QA tracking; Fragmented across systems

5. Push-based stakeholder updates; no self-serve dashboards
6. Post-release surprises due to context gaps

She straightened the papers in front of her with a precise motion, “These are classic observability gaps. Let's architect some ways to illuminate them.”

Recommendations for Observability

1. Implement Context Injection into Strings

Diana began, “Enable automatic **context capture** for strings, such as screenshot snapshots, character limits, gender/number notes embedded directly within the string repository. That eliminates guesswork for translators.”

2. Create End-to-End Localization Dashboards

Reed continued smoothly, “Design dashboards that show localization pipeline status by feature, language, vendor, and phase (handoff, in translation, in review, QA complete). Stakeholders should have self-serve access, not rely on triage.”

3. Automate LQA Defect Logging & Metrics

Diana gestured, “Move LQA issue tracking out of spreadsheets into a system that **auto-categorizes errors**, tracks rework cycles, and visualizes trends over time per locale, content type, and vendor.”

4. Establish Bottleneck Analytics

Reed smiled faintly, "Instrument your workflows with **timestamps at key handoff points**: content freeze, engineering handoff, translation start/complete, QA cycles. You'll get **lead time and cycle time** metrics that pinpoint where delays happen."

5. Introduce Change Traceability

Diana concluded, "Enable **string history logs**: who edited what, when, and why. It builds accountability and helps diagnose regressions."

Suhani sat back, crossing her arms loosely. "We've got some architecture work ahead of us."

Diana's smile was warm but unwavering. "Observability is the lever that turns **anecdotes into data**. And data into decisions."

The daylight had softened by the time we returned to the room. The whiteboard scribbles were fading under the dimmer lights, and empty coffee cups stood like quiet sentinels along the windowsill. Most of the team had drifted back to their regular work, leaving just Ava, Amira, Marco, Nina, Suhani, me, and, of course, Diana and Reed.

Diana closed her notebook gently, the elastic band snapping back over the thick pages that now held three days' worth of sharp observations and field notes.

"Well," Diana began, her gaze lingering on Amira and her voice calm and clear, "I think we've seen enough to understand the shape of things."

Reed, who had been pacing in slow, thoughtful circles for most of the afternoon, finally came to rest near the table, resting his palms on the surface as he spoke. “You know,” he began, glancing between us with a half-smile, “there's a lot of scaffolding here that most companies your size don't have. And believe me, that's not flattery. You've built systems with the real purpose.”

I caught a faint nod from Diana as she echoed, “Yes. Your automation baseline, especially around UI localization, is solid. And the way your teams collaborate, the way context flows, even when imperfect, it's clear this isn't your first time thinking about scale.”

She paused, letting the compliment settle just long enough before shifting her tone.
“But like most organizations that grow fast, your systems have grown a little… uneven. Some areas sprinted ahead. Others, understandably, lagged.”

Reed chimed in, his gaze softening with professional curiosity. “Your integration story is strong where the product surface is predictable. But the non-product content? Marketing, support, legal, even some of your help systems? Those aren't riding the same rails. That's going to pinch later, as you expand.”

Diana tapped her closed notebook lightly with her fingers.
“And on observability, there's visibility, yes. But not enough where it counts most. The translator's desk, the reviewer's screen, your PM's dashboards; there's context missing, and insights hidden under layers of operational noise. Nothing alarming. Just areas where clarity hasn't quite caught up with scale.”

There was no sternness in her words, no dramatic consultant crescendo. Just a steady, confident diagnosis. The kind that made you want to roll up your sleeves, not shrink into your chair.

“We'll take everything we've gathered,” she continued, glancing briefly at Reed, who gave a small nod of agreement, “and distill it into a full audit report. It won't just be observations. We'll map concrete suggestions tailored to your toolchain, workflows, and roadmap. No generic playbook. Only what matches *your* ecosystem.”

Reed smiled then, not the broad grin of a consultant closing a deal, but the relaxed, earned smile of someone who knew their work had landed where it was supposed to, “Think of it as…a calibration document. A guide to align where you are with where you want to be, without tearing apart what already works.”

Diana rose from her chair and stretched slightly, the way someone does after a long hike, tired but satisfied. “We'll send the preliminary draft in two weeks. Plenty of time for you to digest before your next quarterly planning cycle.”

As the room slowly emptied and we all exchanged quiet goodbyes, I couldn't help but notice, in contrast to three days ago, the air didn't feel tense anymore. It felt like a breathing room. Like we'd been handed a mirror not just to see flaws, but to recognize the foundation under our feet.

And sometimes, that's all an audit needs to be.

- - -

Feb 23, 2024

The text came on a Friday afternoon.

“Hey, I'm already at the dentist. Are you guys coming?” Kashika's message popped up, casual as ever, like she was reminding me to pick up a loaf of bread, not that I'd completely forgotten her appointment was today.

I froze. Dentist? Today?

I checked my calendar, nothing. I called Ritu. She checked her calendar. Also, nothing. We'd both been under the impression that the appointment was still weeks away.

Panic

Ritu had Friday blocked off for entirely different errands. I'd booked back-to-back calls, assuming the appointment was later in the month. None of us had accounted for the reschedule.

After a few moments of frantic mental backpedaling, it hit me. The dentist had called to reschedule weeks ago. We'd all nodded, agreed, and then promptly moved on with our lives like it was some sort of adulting victory.

Except, we forgot to actually update the calendars.

Kashika, of course, had updated hers the second she hung up. It's one of the few things she's way better at than I am.

The rest of us? We just kept on as if we had everything together.

Kashika, naturally, handled it like a pro, because why wouldn't she? Still, I felt a little guilty picturing her sitting there all calm and put-together while the rest of us were tripping over each other just to remember a dentist appointment.

And then it hit me, and I had to laugh.

Just a few days earlier, we'd been in that conference room with Diana and Reed, obsessing over workflows, integrations, and visibility, making sure everything was synced, automated, and running like clockwork.

Meanwhile, at home? We were running on that same system where one person vaguely remembers dinner plans while everyone else hopes for the best.

I let out a sigh, half-laughing at the irony.

“Alright, it's time. We need a shared family calendar.”

My Diary Notes

- If localization is *what* we deliver, LocOps is *how* we deliver
- Operational strength stands on four legs: Automate, Integrate, Scale, Observe.
- Integration fails without shared, clean data.
- You can't fix what you can't see.
- Teams grow fast; maturity grows unevenly.

Chapter 10: Governing Scale With Metrics That Count

From Chaos to Clarity

Apr 14, 2024
The late afternoon sun cast long shadows across the tarmac as I checked in at the international terminal. Next stop: London, for our annual **Comventra Global Partner Forum**.

It was one of our flagship events, where we gathered regional partners, merchants, technology vendors, and localization specialists from across continents. Three days of keynotes, strategy sessions, and private roundtables designed to strengthen ties and share our vision for cross-border commerce in the year ahead.

For me, it was more than just a customer connect event. It was a pulse check on how well our globalization efforts were landing in the real world. Our teams had worked tirelessly to launch localized storefronts, integrate regional payments, and streamline multilingual product catalogs, but nothing replaces hearing firsthand from partners in Europe, Asia, and Latin America about what's working and what's getting lost in translation.

With that in mind, I had packed deliberately light: a single carry-on, a slim notebook, and a folder of discussion points for the forum.

Scaling is easy to dream, hard to govern, I thought as I made my way through security.

Several hours later, I settled into seat 3A, a window, my preferred vantage point. The seat leaned back farther than I expected, and the clean linen headrest made it feel like I might actually get some rest over the next ten hours.

A neatly folded menu rested on the side console, and the flight attendant poured sparkling water into a glass tumbler, small signs of comfort I'd come to appreciate on long-haul flights. The man beside me took his seat. Mid-forties, composed, he stowed his briefcase with an air of practiced ease and adjusted his shirt cuffs under a tailored navy blazer.

"Long flight ahead," he remarked, glancing at the seatbelt sign. "Are you heading somewhere for work or just getting away?"

"Yeah, it's going to be a bit of a trek," I said, smiling. "We've got this company event coming up, the Global Partner Forum. We've got partners from all over coming together to discuss how we can deepen cross-border commerce and better support their regional needs."

He nodded appreciatively.
"Sounds interesting! Especially with so many regional dynamics at play. I'm Deepak Mehta, by the way. I work in strategy and analytics, helping organizations navigate global scale using data-driven decision frameworks."

We spent the next hour in easy conversation, covering everything from travel quirks to favorite books, from how technology shapes regional consumer behavior to exchanging tips for managing jet lag.
It wasn't until one particular point Deepak made that my attention sharpened.

He had mentioned, almost in passing, how governance of data becomes one of the most overlooked risks when organizations scale rapidly across multiple markets.

That caught my ear.

He continued, "It's fascinating how companies can have the best systems, workflows, and operational practices, but if the data underpinning all of that isn't structured, aligned, and trusted globally, cracks start showing up: inconsistencies, inefficiencies, even compliance risks."

As he spoke, it hit me.
While at Comventra, we had made strong progress in Internationalization Engineering, Localization Engineering, Localization Operations, and QA, we hadn't deeply considered data governance as a scaling lever. We had solid workflows. But was our data equally robust, consistent, and reliable across every market and partner ecosystem?
That realization quietly took root as Deepak elaborated, pulling in ideas from his work that had shaped his thinking.

The Challenge of Scaling without Data Governance

Flying high over western Canada, I watched the forests and clouds drift by below, the engines purring in the background like a steady reminder of distance.

Deepak's tone shifted slightly, moving from observation to something closer to conviction, "Here's the thing, Sourabh. As organizations scale, the sheer volume of decisions, markets, and moving parts creates a fog. Without clear, shared metrics and accountable ownership, it gets harder and harder to tell what's actually happening. You lose clarity on what's working, where the bottlenecks are, or whether teams are pulling in the same direction."

He rested his coffee cup down gently, "I've seen it across industries. Teams start building local adaptations, regional definitions creep in, and leadership dashboards start contradicting each other. People don't know which numbers to trust. And trust me, alignment unravels faster than anyone expects when that happens."

I nodded slowly, a familiar undercurrent surfacing in my mind.

At Comventra, we had architected solid internationalization guardrails, reliable localization workflows, integrated LocOps, and mature QA. On the surface, everything was humming. But as Deepak spoke, a subtle unease stirred.

Had we defined and governed our globalization data with the same rigor?

Were we certain that the definition of "localized product readiness" meant the same thing across EMEA and APAC? Did our partner dashboards in Brazil tell the same story as those in Germany?
And when regional leads pulled data for quarterly reviews, were we confident they were comparing apples to apples?

Deepak continued, almost reading my mind, "Data governance sounds dry, but it's the connective tissue at scale. When the business spans countries and cultures, your operations and your insights depend on shared, trusted definitions and clear ownership. Without it, complexity multiplies quietly."

He sat back, thoughtful for a moment, "You can't scale what you can't see or measure."

The words landed heavier than he perhaps intended.

It wasn't that we lacked data. It was that in an increasingly global landscape, the consistency, alignment, and stewardship of that data were what would determine whether we scaled smoothly or stumbled over mismatches.

I found myself leaning forward, more curious now than ever.

Setting Clear, Aligned Goals

I shifted slightly in my seat, setting my glass of water back on the tray table. "I'm starting to wonder," I said, glancing toward Deepak, "how do companies make sure all their teams stay aligned when they're expanding this quickly? It's one thing to have a strategy, but executing it across functions is a whole other beast."

Deepak gave a knowing smile, as if he'd heard the same question echo across boardrooms many times before, "You're right. That's the crux of scaling, not just growing fast, but growing coherently."

He paused for a moment, then added, "One of the most powerful levers we've leaned on in my organization is OKRs. Objectives and Key Results."

I nodded slowly, "I've heard the term, but I can't say we've formally embraced them."

He nodded, "Yes, that's them. They're not just a buzzword, though. When done right, OKRs force clarity. They make you articulate not just what you're aiming for, the Objective, but how you'll know you're making real progress, the Key Results."

He tapped gently on the tray table with two fingers, emphasizing his point, "The beauty is in their simplicity. Objectives set direction; Key Results create measurability. And when teams from different functions all align to shared OKRs, you get focus, alignment, and often surprisingly, a healthy stretch that pushes everyone just a notch further than their comfort zone."

The question surfaced before I could stop it, "How does that look in practice? Can you give me an example?"

Deepak smiled, "Sure. In my company, we were expanding our supply chain footprint into emerging markets a couple of years ago. The overarching Objective was *'Ensure seamless global supply chain operations in three new markets within 12 months.'*
He lifted his hand and began counting off on his fingers, one by one, "The Key Results underneath were sharp and measurable:
First, onboard three regional logistics partners with 95% SLA adherence.
Second, localize inventory management workflows for compliance in all target countries.
Third, achieve 98% data consistency across regional and global inventory dashboards."

He paused, letting the example sink in, "What it did was align operations, engineering, partner management, and compliance teams toward one unifying goal, each with their slice of measurable impact."

I sat back in my seat, the wheels in my mind turning.

At Comventra, we had many well-oiled parts: engineering, localization operations, QA, and more. Each had their own roadmaps and KPIs, but…

Were they bound tightly enough around clear, shared objectives?

I could think of instances where engineering had advanced features for new markets, but localization or QA lagged slightly behind, not for lack of effort but due to misaligned priorities or differing timelines.

"I can see how that could apply to globalization, too," I mused aloud. "We've been scaling aggressively: multiple markets, multiple partners. We have solid systems and processes in place. But maybe we don't always define sharp, cross-functional goals that tie Engineering, LocOps, and QA together in the same measurable direction."

Deepak nodded approvingly, "Hmm. OKRs shine in cross-functional complexity. When teams naturally drift apart because their day-to-day lenses are different, shared OKRs anchor everyone to common outcomes."

He reached into the seat pocket and pulled out a pen, scribbling something on the back of a napkin, "Think of it like this," he said, sliding the napkin toward me:

Vision → Objectives → Key Results → Team Actions

"Each layer sharpens the focus. And data governance? That's what makes the Key Results trustworthy."

I smiled, already picturing how something like this could streamline some of our globalization rollout complexities.

"This is giving me a lot to think about," I admitted.

"That's the idea," Deepak replied with a grin. "Scaling isn't about more teams doing more things. It's about teams doing the right things, together, with visibility."

As Deepak laid out his Key Results, something clicked for me.

I glanced at Deepak and said, "Mind if I jot a few notes down? This is sparking some ideas for my team that I don't want to lose."
He nodded with a knowing smile.

I reached down and pulled my tablet from the seat pocket. I opened a blank email draft and began sketching the thoughts out. Nothing formal. Just a rough outline of how OKRs might sharpen alignment across our globalization teams.

Email draft (on screen):

Subject: Draft OKRs: Globalization Alignment

Objective: Deliver fully global-ready releases in five key regions within six months.

Key Results:
- Integrate i18n coverage into 100% of core codebases.
- Complete localization of all tier-1 features within two weeks of feature freeze.
- Achieve <1% localization-related defects in LQA for all target languages.

I didn't add any recipients. The draft would sit in my outbox until I'd had time to refine it properly. The last thing I wanted was to send a half-baked strategy from 38,000 feet.

I locked the screen, my mind still turning over the possibilities.

Measuring the Intangibles

I set the tablet aside and leaned back, satisfied that the draft email could wait for review later. As I adjusted the small reading light above us, Deepak glanced at me thoughtfully.

"You know," he began, "one thing we realized pretty late in our journey was how much of what matters most… isn't obvious to measure."

I nodded slowly. "Like what? Aren't most metrics just… well, numbers? You measure what's countable, no?"

He gave a small smile. "That's the default assumption. But that's where *How to Measure Anything* by Douglas Hubbard really shifted my thinking. The author's argument is simple but powerful; even seemingly fuzzy, intangible things can be quantified. You just need the right proxies or leading indicators."

A flight attendant passed by quietly, placing a small bowl of warm nuts between us with a polite nod. I absentmindedly reached for a few as Deepak continued.

"For example, in one of our data governance projects, we were trying to gauge something tricky, our *organization's culture around data quality*. How much did people value data accuracy and consistency in their day-to-day work? You can't exactly run a SQL query and get an answer to that," he chuckled.

I tilted my head, intrigued. "So, what did you do?"

"We found proxies," He tapped his fingers lightly on the armrest, counting them off, "Things like:
- The frequency with which teams flagged bad data upstream, not just fixed downstream.
- Participation rates in data quality training sessions.

- How often dashboards and reports had annotations or metadata explaining sources and transformations."

"Individually small signals… but together? A pretty decent indicator of whether a data quality mindset existed."

I sat back, letting that sink in. The idea made sense. A proxy didn't have to be perfect or absolute. It just had to be *good enough* to show a trend, to shed light on something otherwise invisible.

"You know," I said slowly, "we've always wrestled with how to measure things like *translation quality* or *cultural relevance*. We have standard linguistic QA scores, sure… but that doesn't always tell us if users feel the product 'speaks their language' beyond literal words."

Deepak's eyes lit up. "Exactly. That's where proxies come in. Maybe it's user feedback trends by market. Or how often local teams escalate content mismatches. Or the ratio of translator queries about missing context. That's a clue about upstream clarity."

I leaned forward, warmed by the thought. "Or even something like *time-to-resolve* for localization bugs that are cultural, not technical."

He nodded approvingly. "Yes. The point is… lack of direct measurement doesn't mean lack of measurability. It just means we need to get creative."

Outside, soft streaks of twilight lined the horizon. We were well into our transatlantic stretch now. Somewhere below, the endless ocean reflected faint glimmers of the setting sun.

I rubbed my chin thoughtfully. “Maybe it's time we reframed how we measure quality and cultural fit globally, not just bugs and word counts.”

I reached for the tablet again, but this time didn't type. Instead, I simply opened a blank note and titled it ‘Proxy Indicators - Globalization'. Just a seed, for later.

Embedding Analytics into Globalization Workflows

The seatbelt sign pinged softly overhead, and a flight attendant glided past us with a tray of drinks, with her calm and practiced movements. I declined the offer with a smile and turned back to Deepak. The cabin had settled into a muted hum now. Engines steady, window shades half-drawn, screens glowing softly around us.

Deepak's smartwatch gave a quiet buzz. He glanced down, tapped it once, and smiled faintly.

“Even midair, our systems keep nudging me,” he said, anticipating my glance. “Looks like one of our regional dashboards flagged an inventory discrepancy in our Southeast Asia hub. The supply chain monitoring tool had queued it before we took off. Smart enough to sync offline and alert me just now.”

His gaze drifted toward the window, reflective. “That's what we learned the hard way, Sourabh. Metrics don't drive decisions if they live in siloed reports or quarterly decks. They need to live *inside* the tools where work happens, so when something drifts off course, people know instantly and can act. No delays. No surprises.”

I nodded slowly.
"Embedded analytics," I said aloud, more to myself than to him.

"Yes. Analytics embedded in the tools." Deepak affirmed. "We don't ask teams to generate status reports manually every week. Instead, dashboards are baked directly into our ERP system, supplier portals, and even our messaging tools. So, whether it's a logistics delay or a compliance breach, people *see* it in context and act fast."

I mulled over his words, drumming my fingers lightly on my armrest.

"You know," I said after a pause, "in globalization, we tend to think of metrics as retrospective artifacts. Reports someone pulls at the end of a sprint, or post-mortem stats after a market launch. But embedding them directly into our Localization and Engineering workflows…"
I trailed off, the implications clicking into place.

Deepak smiled knowingly. "Now you're thinking."

I sat up straighter, reaching for my tablet on the tray table.
"Let's play this out. If I think of ShopSphere's globalization workflows: engineering, localization, QA, PMO, what kinds of dashboards *should* live in their daily tools?" I asked, sketching as I spoke.

Deepak nodded, encouraging.

"Well," I began, "for Engineering, something like an i18n Code Coverage dashboard embedded right into our CI/CD pipeline. So, every time a build runs, we'd see what % of code paths are internationalized properly."

I flipped to a new page on my tablet.
"For our Localization Ops team, a Translation Progress and Quality dashboard directly inside the TMS. No more emailing spreadsheets back and forth; they can see real-time progress, quality flags, glossary adherence, all at a glance."

Interest flickered in Arjun's eyes. "And for PMO?"

I smiled. "A Market Launch Readiness dashboard. Pulling data from all streams: code readiness, localization completion, LQA pass rates, legal approvals, so program managers see a single, unified view of whether a locale is ready to ship."

He tapped the armrest appreciatively. "There you go. And you don't have to boil the ocean either. *Lean Analytics*, the book by Alistair Croll and Benjamin Yoskovitz, pushes that idea hard. One metric that matters per stage. Just enough to trigger action. Not overload."

I nodded again, jotting a final note on my screen:
Embed actionable, real-time, contextual metrics → into daily globalization workflows.
I capped my stylus upon hearing a calm voice crackle over the intercom.

"Ladies and gentlemen, this is your captain speaking. We'll be encountering a short stretch of turbulence shortly. Please ensure your seatbelts are fastened."

I tucked my tablet back and clipped the belt as the aircraft shuddered gently. Somehow, though, the slight bumpiness matched the shift in my own thinking, a little turbulence that was shaking loose old patterns, making space for sharper, embedded ways of working.

Continuous Conversations & Feedback Loops

I slid the in-flight magazine out of the seat pocket. Flipping past travel ads and destination guides, I paused on a page. It was an airline ad asking passengers to share feedback about their flight experience: a simple survey link paired with a smiling crew photo.

I smiled faintly and murmured, "They really want to know what we think, huh?"

Deepak glanced over at the page and nodded. "Smart move. Regular feedback like that... it keeps companies sharp. We used something similar in one of our programs, not just surveys, but real back-and-forth conversations. It made a surprising difference."

I tilted my head, curious. "Back-and-forth as in customer interviews?"

"Wider than that," he said. He set his coffee cup down gently on the tray table. "We borrowed a model called CFRs: Conversations, Feedback, and Recognition. John Doerr popularized it in his work on goal setting, as a complement to OKRs. The idea is that, beyond hard metrics, you need structured but regular dialogues to stay aligned. Weekly syncs, quick retrospectives, even small shoutouts when something goes right. It sounds simple, but it prevents drift and builds trust."

Deepak continued, "When we rolled this out, it wasn't formal or heavy. Just rhythms like:
- Weekly 15-minute syncs across our cross-functional teams
- Short retrospectives after key rollouts
- Feedback loops that included not just execs, but people on the ground - partners, customers, vendors"

He smiled. “And recognition. That's the part most people forget. Celebrating small wins, even just an email shoutout, kept the team energized.”

I nodded slowly, the idea landing but not fully settling. My brow furrowed, curiosity sparking. “Okay… but how does that actually look in practice?”

Arjun paused, his brow furrowing in thought. “Let me give you an example from one of my past teams. We built data infrastructure tools. Our OKR for that quarter was clear: *'Improve data pipeline reliability to 99.9% uptime.'* Straightforward, measurable. But here's the thing. Halfway through the quarter, we hit unexpected snags. Legacy systems, third-party APIs flaking out, and even a surprise dependency we hadn't accounted for.”

He paused as the attendant gently handed him a glass of water.

“Now, if we had only been tracking OKRs, those issues would've surfaced too late, maybe at the end of the quarter review. Instead, because we had weekly CFRs, the engineers and product managers had standing one-on-ones and small team huddles. Conversations flagged the roadblocks early. Feedback flowed in both ways, engineers shared concerns, and PMs adjusted timelines. And importantly…”, he tapped the edge of his glass, “…we recognized quick wins every week. Someone fixed the API retry logic? They got called out. We successfully rerouted a flaky service? We celebrated.”

I could see where he was going.
“Kept morale up even when things got messy,” I said quietly.

“Right.” He smiled. “By the end of the quarter, no, we didn't hit exactly 99.9%, but we got to 99.7%, with no burnout and no surprises. The team felt informed, appreciated, and aligned the whole way.”

I scribbled fast on my tablet, ideas spinning now. In globalization, it's rarely a straight road either. Market-specific content changes, translation bottlenecks, region-specific compliance issues…
Regular CFRs could surface these earlier *and* keep everyone motivated.

I put the magazine down and tapped my tablet awake, "I wonder what this could look like for globalization work…"

I started jotting:

Possible CFRs for Globalization:

- Weekly Globalization Syncs: align Engineering, LocOps, Marketing
- Post-Launch Retrospectives: what went well, what to improve (per locale)
- Feedback Channels: from translators, regional SMEs, in-market customers
- Celebrate Milestones: first locale launch, zero-bug releases, translator kudos

I looked up. "This would help us course-correct before a market launch goes sideways. Not just after."

Deepak nodded approvingly. "Exactly. Metrics tell you *what* is happening. Conversations tell you *why*. You need both."

I locked the tablet screen and sat back, the ideas quietly settling. Embedding steady conversations into our globalization work suddenly felt not just possible, but necessary.

Governing Data Quality & Ownership

The engines rumbled steadily beneath us, a low, constant hum that seemed to give space for deeper thought. I tapped my tablet awake, scrolling back through our notes from earlier.

"You know," I started, almost thinking aloud, "we've been talking a lot about analytics, dashboards, metrics… but that only works if the data behind them is trustworthy."

Deepak tilted his head, brows raised slightly in invitation. "Go on."

"I mean…" I sat straighter, warming up to the idea. "It's one thing to collect numbers. It's another thing to be confident that those numbers are accurate and up to date. If not, we'll end up making decisions based on incomplete or bad data. That could do more harm than good."

Deepak nodded slowly. "True. And what would make the data trustworthy?"

"Well…" I hesitated, frowning slightly. "I guess… someone should own each data stream? I don't mean a heavy governance committee. Just… accountability embedded into normal workflows."

"Not bad," Deepak said evenly. "But you're skating close to abstract. Can you make it more concrete?"

I exhaled through my nose, organizing my thoughts. "Alright. For example:
Our Program Manager already curates OKR dashboards for project tracking.
Our Lead Engineer keeps tabs on i18n code coverage stats from CI/CD pipelines.
Our Localization Specialist monitors translation quality

through the TMS.
If we explicitly say those are *their* metrics to maintain, it's not extra work, it's just formally recognized ownership."

Deepak's eyes narrowed thoughtfully, nodding. "Better. You're describing data stewardship embedded within roles. You just need to avoid fuzziness. Be clear about scope and cadence."

"Right." I tapped a quick note on my tablet. "For each metric, we could define:

Metric → Owner → Usage → Review cadence."

"Good," Deepak confirmed. "And cadence?"

"Well…" I chewed my lip. "Program Manager might review dashboards bi-weekly during PMO check-ins. Engineer updates code coverage after every sprint. Localization Specialist refreshes translation quality monthly… something like that?"

Deepak raised a hand, pausing me gently. "Careful. Don't leave it at 'something like that'. *Be exact*. Review cadence isn't just a guess; it needs to match how fast the underlying data changes and how often decisions depend on it."

I nodded slowly, absorbing that. "So… sprint-based data → sprint review. Quarterly data → quarterly review. Match rhythms."

"Doesn't it?" His voice carried the steady conviction of experience. "That's the essence of non-invasive data governance, clarity without bureaucracy."

He paused for a second, then added, “Ever come across *Non-Invasive Data Governance* by Bob Seiner?”

I shook my head.

“It's a slim book, but deceptively sharp,” Deepak continued. “Seiner argues that traditional data governance often fails because it tries to impose heavy new processes on top of how people already work. His approach flips that: instead of creating new roles or committees, you formalize the responsibility people already have. You recognize the natural stewards of data in their existing jobs and give them the visibility and support to manage it explicitly.”

Curiosity stirred again.

“So,” Deepak clarified, “your Program Manager already watches OKRs? You just say: ‘That's your data domain.' Your engineer already monitors code coverage. Right? You make it clear it's part of their stewardship.
Minimal disruption, maximum clarity.”

I tapped a note briskly. “That's… clean. Feels respectful of how people work, but still tight enough to avoid chaos.”

Deepak smiled. “Exactly why I like the approach. You're not delegating new work; you're simply acknowledging existing accountability. Makes adoption easier.”

I nodded slowly, the concept settling in. Not adding a process but making responsibility visible.

As the cabin lights dimmed, clarity settled in quietly.

We didn't need heavy governance at Comventra, just thoughtful stewardship, woven seamlessly into the work we were already doing.

- - -

The hours had drifted by. Our conversations had woven in and out, like gentle currents, interspersed with stretches of quiet, naps, and the rhythm of long-haul travel.

I scrolled back through my tablet notes, the screen dim in the soft cabin light. Metrics, feedback loops, ownership… fragments of frameworks and ideas neatly captured, yet clearly only the starting point.

I glanced once at my notes and smiled faintly. Naren's words echoed in the back of my mind. His constant refrain was that governance wasn't about control, but about creating clarity for teams to move faster. What Deepak and I discussed today felt like another step toward that same ideal.

And somehow, as if by quiet design, Deepak had appeared at just the right moment, offering exactly the kind of wisdom, very important but I hadn't known I needed.

As the wheels touched down and the runway lights blurred past the window, I tucked the tablet away with quiet resolve. I had enough to start a thoughtful conversation with my team, and enough questions left to shape it together.

As we landed and turned off the seatbelt signs, my phone pinged with a message from the family group. The photo they shared showed them gathered around the dinner table. And a message, "Can't wait for you to be back, Dad!"

It reminded me that, while global challenges were at the forefront of my mind, the world I was building for my family was just as important.

Note: While this chapter focused more on the principles behind governance and ownership, it's essential to remember that the full spectrum of globalization metrics is broad. For anyone looking to dive deeper, I've included a comprehensive list of suggested metrics in the Appendix III: Globalization & Localization Metrics, ranging from commonly tracked indicators like locale launch readiness to more advanced ones like global user sentiment tracking."

—

My Diary Notes

- Clarity speeds up teams more than control does.
- Data without trust is noise.
- Ownership shines brighter when it's lightweight.
- Stewardship beats centralization.
- Responsibility sticks when embedded in roles.
- Measure only what you're willing to act on.
- Governance is guidance, not gatekeeping.
- Visibility prevents rework.
- A metric unloved is a metric unused.
- Right owners make the right data matter.
- Make ownership visible.
- Metrics are mirrors, not scorecards.
- Small, clear accountabilities scale faster than big committees.
- Governance flows best when it fits the way people already work.
- Sometimes the right counsel arrives uninvited, but perfectly timed.

Chapter 11: Use of AI

Augmenting Globalization with Intelligence

Terms you need to know	
Term	**Definition**
Model drift	Changes in an AI model's behavior or output over time, often due to updated training data or architecture changes, leading to inconsistencies.
Sandboxed environment	A restricted and controlled computing setup where software runs with limited access, used to isolate execution and prevent security risks.
Prompt templates	Pre-defined and structured input formats designed to guide large language models toward reliable, consistent, and safe responses.
Anti-patterns	Common but flawed coding practices that can cause maintainability, performance, or security issues, especially in internationalization.
Open-weight models	AI models whose trained parameters are openly available, allowing users to run them locally or customize them for specific use cases.
On-prem	Short for "on-premises"; refers to deploying and running software or models on the organization's own servers instead of using cloud services.
Visual heuristics	Rule-based visual cues used to detect layout or UI issues, such as text truncation or misalignment, often in localization testing.
Appium	An open-source testing tool used to automate mobile applications across iOS and Android platforms.
Shadow mode	A deployment technique where a new system runs alongside the live system without affecting users, used for safe testing and comparison.
Product taxonomy	The structured classification of products into categories and attributes, used to ensure consistent labeling, translation, and content handling.

By the time I walked into the open-floor conference zone, the folding chairs were arranged in a half-moon, and the snack trays were already under siege. A hand-sketched sign read

"GlobalHack: Intelligence Unleashed", and someone had scribbled *"(within reason)"* underneath it. I didn't need handwriting analysis to know it was Lorenzo.
This wasn't a stakeholder sync or a roadmap kickoff. No slides. No Kanban boards. Just a strange blend of buzz and focus, like the room had collectively agreed to suspend disbelief, at least for the Last 48 hours. The final hours of the hackathon had arrived.
Around me sat a mix of engineers, localization leads, QA specialists, designers, and PMs. Over the past month, they'd been given space, some officially, some sneakily between sprints to come up with AI ideas that could help us scale globalization faster, smarter, and safer.
Now, it was time to bring those ideas to light.
Lorenzo stood near the whiteboard, sipping from his chipped mug like a man about to open both a hackathon and a sermon. He caught my eye and grinned.

"Just in time," he said. "This whole thing was your idea anyway."
I nodded, letting him take the floor.

He turned to the team, raised his voice just enough to ride the quiet hum of anticipation, and began.
"Folks. Thanks for showing up physically, mentally, and for some of you, even emotionally. You've had a month to cook up ideas, argue with yourselves, and probably get weird looks from coworkers when you said 'I'm teaching an agent to fail in Basque.'"

A chuckle rippled through the group.

"We're in the middle of an AI wave. Assistants are writing code, bots are answering customers, and translation engines are doing in seconds what used to take weeks. But here's the thing:

this isn't about riding hype. This is about asking, what's AI good for *here*?"

He pointed at the floor for emphasis.

"Globalization, as you know, is about subtlety, timing, adaptability, and context. It's a game of precision and empathy. If we get it wrong, we're not just pushing a bad release, we're pushing cultural disrespect."
He paused, then turned and wrote on the whiteboard in bold block letters:
Transparency.
Safety.
Human-in-the-loop.

"We have been talking about these principles to guide you through your ideation and prototyping. If it can't explain itself, we don't deploy it. If it fails silently, we walk away. If it takes the place of human judgment without human supervision, it's a no-go."
He underlined the words once, then turned back around.
"The Hackathon's over," he said, his voice steady with that familiar post-sprint calm. "Months of ideas, two days of hard work, and no sleep. Now it's time for the presentations. Ideas, ready to be honed and greenlit for real development, with a tight scope and clear timelines."
He smiled, the energy in the room still buzzing around him.
"You've not just been here to prototype. You've shaped how we'll globalize smarter, faster, and without losing what matters. So, let's get into it."
He smiled again, half excitement, half dare. "You're not just here to prototype. You're here to shape how we globalize smarter, faster, and without compromising what matters. So. Let's get started."
He capped the marker. "Who's first?"

Idea 1: Machine Translation: From NMT to LLM
Priya Iyer, the L10n Engineering Lead, stepped up confidently, a laptop in hand. Kenji Sato, her I18N specialist partner, followed closely behind and began sharing their demo on the big screen.
Priya wasted no time. “We’ve been using Neural Machine Translation, or NMT as we call it, for quite a while. It’s reliable, fast, and scales well. But it has its limitations, especially when it comes to translating context or nuanced language. Our idea is to explore how we can incorporate large language models or LLMs into specific parts of our localization pipeline to boost quality and precision.”
She quickly switched to a side-by-side comparison chart on the screen.”We ran controlled tests on a batch of 100 live production strings: UI copy, marketing text, and even some long-form content. First, we used NMT, then we tried LLM. We had a group of bilingual QA testers assess both sets.”

Kenji took over.”What we found: NMT still holds strong where content is formulaic or format-sensitive. But LLMs perform significantly better in handling idioms, cultural references, and long-tail phrases that require more than a word-for-word translation.”

I leaned in, trying to grasp the full scope of it.”You’re saying LLMs can pick up on tone and meaning, but we’d still need NMT for highly structured content?”

“Exactly,” Priya confirmed. “LLMs shine where human-like judgment is needed. For instance, user-facing content like marketing copy, hero banners, and error messages are the perfect candidates for LLMs.”

Kenji added, “But LLMs can be slower, and they come with a higher cost when we’re looking at scaling translations. That’s why we propose a hybrid approach. Use NMT for structured

content like buttons, labels, form fields, and deploy LLMs where nuance matters."
I rubbed my chin thoughtfully. "What about latency and cost, though?"

"We can optimize it," Priya said. "By batching requests and caching the translations we use most frequently, we can keep the cost down and the latency within acceptable limits. We'll need a monitoring strategy to scale the solution intelligently."

Priya switched to an example from one of their recent projects. On the screen, a marketing campaign headline appeared:

"Hurry! Limited time only: Big Discounts for You!"

Kenji highlighted the translations produced by both NMT and LLM.
"Here's where NMT falls short," Kenji said, zooming in on the LLM translation: "¡Date prisa! ¡Descuentos enormes solo para ti!"

"See," Priya pointed at the LLM translation. "NMT was stuck translating the literal meaning of 'Big Discounts for You.' But the LLM picked up the context, 'Hurry!', 'Limited time', and 'for You', and translated it into a more natural, engaging sentence that's both culturally relevant and appropriate for Spanish-speaking users."

Lorenzo leaned forward, impressed. "That's a huge improvement over our old campaigns. We've had cases where the translated content felt too rigid or uninspired."

"Exactly," Priya replied. "LLMs handle these subtleties much better. And the best part is, as we gather more data, we can tune our models for even higher accuracy."

As the room settled, I leaned in slightly. "Let's walk through this using the principles we agreed to. First up, **transparency**. How are you tracking what the model does?"

Priya didn't miss a beat. "Every interaction with the LLM is logged. We tag each translated segment with the prompt, model version, and a confidence score. That way, we have complete visibility into what was generated, when, and how."

Lorenzo gave a nod, but his expression turned more serious. "Okay, but what about **safety**? Can these models be trusted with user-facing content, especially if it includes sensitive data?"
Kenji responded, calm and deliberate. "We've designed the system to fail safely. Inputs are tightly controlled. There's no dynamic user content passed to the model, no customer addresses, no payment info, no order history, and definitely no health records or internal support tickets. The LLM runs in a sandboxed environment, with pre-approved prompt templates and scrubbed inputs only."

I glanced at Suhani, who had been quietly taking notes. Her team had caught enough localization bugs to know what was at stake. "And human-in-the-loop?"

"Mandatory," Priya replied. "Every LLM-generated string goes through human QA before it touches production, at least for the pilot. Down the line, if the prompt designs and output behavior stabilize, we may shift to post-deployment reviews. But right now, nothing goes live without human eyes on it."

Lorenzo leaned back slightly, a half-smile on his face. "So this would've saved us from that infamous Japan campaign?"

A ripple of low laughter moved through the room. No one had forgotten the stiff, robotic phrasing that had made the promo read like a tax notice.

"Absolutely," Priya said. "Back then, we let raw machine translation through without tone checks or context alignment. With this system, we could've used custom prompts that adapt tone and intent. It would've flagged the awkwardness before anyone hit publish."

Lorenzo tilted his head slightly. "This is solid work," he said, directing the room's attention back to Priya and Kenji. "But let's widen the lens a bit. These models, while impressive, aren't infallible. What happens when the LLM gets something wrong?"

Kenji didn't flinch. "We've seen that. In one of our dry runs, the model confidently translated a line from a marketing email and injected urgency that wasn't there. It invented a 'limited-time offer' that never existed."

"That's a hallucination," Priya added. "And when you're dealing with price, policy, or legal content, even small inaccuracies can break trust."
You leaned forward. "What about model drift? We've seen inconsistent tone in previous versions of machine translation systems, especially after updates."

"We've accounted for that," Priya said. "Every prompt has version control. Outputs are tagged with the model used and a confidence score. If anything misfires, we can trace and revert."

Across the table, Amira spoke up. "Are you folding this into our standard CI/CD?"

Kenji answered, "Yes. We're drafting an engineering checklist that lives alongside our deployment pipeline. Every use of LLMs goes through it, data scope, prompt design, test coverage, fallback logic."

Lorenzo leaned back in his chair. "That's one thing we got wrong a couple of months ago. The pricing FAQ was mistranslated in Dutch. We didn't have any real traceability."

A few heads nodded. The memory still stung.

Priya smiled. "With the LLM approach, we can finally build translation pipelines that are traceable, versioned, and safe by design."

I was making my Notes:

- **NMT for high-volume, structure-heavy content** (e.g., buttons, labels).
- **LLMs for nuanced, high-impact content** (e.g., marketing, error messages).
- Build a **control framework** with prompt validation, caching, and human QA.
- **Context gaps**: Reduced via prompt templates and locked versions.
- **Hallucinations**: Addressed by human QA and confidence scoring.
- **Inconsistency across model versions**: Managed through output tagging and version control.
- **Engineering guardrails**: Codified via CI/CD checklist before deployment.

The conversation wound down, and the team wrapped up their deck. The proposal had a solid spine, guardrails were built in, risks acknowledged, and it hit the right balance between ambition and responsibility.

We had agreed not to share our verdicts until the end of the hackathon. But as Lorenzo stood up to stretch, he left his notebook slightly ajar on the table. I caught an accidental glimpse of the page.
In the corner, underlined twice in his slanted script, were three words:
"Approved for pilot."
I smiled quietly to myself.
That was exactly my verdict, too.

Idea 2: AI-Powered Code Assessment
The room hadn't lost momentum, but the mood had shifted slightly: focused, grounded.
Diego stood next, flanked by Mei and Samuel. He adjusted his hoodie sleeves like he was stepping into a ring, then clicked to a slide that looked more like a battlefield than a presentation: a messy chunk of JavaScript code.
"Let me introduce you to something familiar," he said, tone dry. "Legacy i18n debt. Or, as we sometimes call it... global sabotage."
Laughter rolled through the room, equal parts humor and the sting of recognition.
The screen showed this gem:

```
const message = "Only " + remaining + " items left! Order before " + new Date().toLocaleDateString();
```

Mei stepped in. "At a glance, it seems fine, right? Until you try to ship it to Germany or Japan. Date format? Broken. Pluralization? Awkward. Word order? English-dependent. This isn't just unlocalized, it's unlocalizable."
"What we're proposing," Diego said, "is an AI-powered assessment tool for i18n code hygiene. Not just string extraction or pseudo-localization. We're talking context-aware detection of anti-patterns, with explainable suggestions."

Samuel chimed in, "LLMs are great at catching nuance. This one flags issues, tells you why, and proposes a safer structure. Like here," he clicked again, revealing a refactor:

```
const message =
i18n.t("itemsRemainingMessage", { count:
remaining, deadline: deadlineDate });
```

"And the key," Mei added, "uses ICU MessageFormat with plural rules, and passes a timestamp, not a formatted string. This can now work in Arabic, French, Japanese, you name it."

I thought instantly of the product launch a few quarters back, where a hardcoded weekday name went out untranslated to five markets. That escalation had nearly cost us an entire sprint.

What struck me wasn't just the tool, but how they'd rooted it in our principles. The AI wasn't rewriting code; it was shining a light. Engineers stayed in control. The AI surfaced blind spots.

Still, I raised a hand. "What about hallucinations? We've seen models fix what isn't broken, and confidently."

Mei nodded. "It's a risk, for sure. We treat the model like a senior reviewer, smart, but not infallible."

Samuel broke down their guardrails:

- **No automatic refactors**: everything runs in dry-run mode.
- **Every suggestion comes with a confidence score and an explanation.**
- **The diffs are reviewed manually in the PR**, with LLM-generated context embedded in the description.
  And anything user-facing gets gated by an L10N tag.

Diego added, "Also, we've locked the model and the prompts. Same as how we pin dependencies. If we upgrade, it triggers a full regression test and prompts validation."

Lorenzo leaned forward, his voice calm but direct. "But in our setup, with strict code privacy, work is done in secure domes. How do we make that work?"

Samuel didn't miss a beat. "We expected that question. For teams like ours that can't use cloud inference, we've run the prototype with open-weight models, StarCoder, and Code LLaMA, completely on-prem. You get the same functionality, just more control. And for extra safety, we've built in preprocessing steps to redact sensitive identifiers before any analysis happens. The code stays private, secure, and compliant with our internal policies."

I appreciated how calmly he said it. We'd had enough debate around LLMs and privacy to last a fiscal quarter. It mattered that they had answers.

Their final example landed with a quiet punch: a checkout flow that had assumed English's month-day format and completely failed during a UK Mother's Day promotion. The model had flagged it and even suggested abstracting the logic into a locale-aware date utility.

I flipped open my notebook.
LLMs detect i18n anti-patterns in legacy and new code, flag with reasons.

Hallucinations: Tackled with confidence scoring and human-in-the-loop PR reviews, augmentation over automation
Upgrades: Prompts versioned, locked, and treated like code dependencies.
Privacy and security: Cloud APIs for prototyping; open-weight models like StarCoder used on-prem in secure org setups.
Usage: Could've saved us a four-day rollback in Q2, can quickly help code assessment with new products onboarded.
I glanced up as they returned to their seats.

"Approved for pilot"

Idea 3: Agentic AI for LQA

This time, it was Aisha Bahar who rose. Tall, calm, with an engineer's poise and a designer's eye, she didn't speak right away. She let the silence breathe, flipping open her laptop and casting the next slide onto the screen.

"Localization Testing: Meet Your New Lab Partner."

She turned to us with a measured smile. "I want to talk about the moment right after we localize. When we think we're done. When the translated strings look good in a spreadsheet, but on screen… they break. Overflow. Truncation. Mistranslation. UI wrap disasters that sneak past our eyes until a user in São Paulo screenshots it and tags us on social media."

A few chuckles. A few knowing groans.

Aisha tapped her keyboard. The next slide was a carousel of familiar pain: French text spilling out of buttons, German breaking the layout grid, Chinese characters smashed by pixel clipping.

"Visual regression testing for localization is a bear," she said. "Manual screenshots, inconsistent coverage, and honestly… we miss things. So here's our pitch: an agentic AI system, trained to act like a localization-aware tester."

Jin Park chimed in from beside her. "Think of it as a virtual QA engineer with a photographic memory and no fatigue. The agent loads the localized app, runs scripted flows, takes screenshots, and here's the kicker, flags issues based on visual heuristics, locale rules, and even past defects."

He clicked again. “We trained the agent on our own bug archive. Remember the checkout flow that broke in Finnish? It caught the same pattern in our staging build last week. Proactively.”

“That’s not all,” Aisha added. “The agent understands the linguistic layer, too. We’ve integrated language model checks for terminology consistency, right-to-left alignment issues, gender mismatches, and even tone inconsistency. It flags when a formal string slips into informal, based on locale norms.”
I leaned forward, already thinking of the Latin American campaign last quarter, where the Spanish translation in the hero banner used Castilian vocabulary instead of Latin American colloquialisms. Nobody caught it until day three. This could’ve flagged it in staging.
Lorenzo spoke before I could. “This is sharp. But what about false positives? And platform compatibility? Does the agent work across mobile, web, and native apps?”

Jin nodded. “We’ve containerized the testing agent, javascript based testing for browser, Appium for mobile. Each test run produces a visual diff, a defect report, and a linguistic validation sheet.”

Aisha added, “And we’ve tuned the model with guardrails:
It never files issues directly.
Every flagged issue gets a confidence score
Any content-related issue routes to the L10N team for review.
It also checks for string reuse, flags where reused keys might create contextually incorrect translations.”

I asked, “And how do you avoid model drift? What if the detection gets noisier with time?”
Jin smiled. “We version both the testing heuristic rules and the language models used. Model upgrades run in shadow mode

first. And we cross-check any shift in detection rates with past stable runs."

"And privacy?" I asked. "Our staging builds aren't always stripped of customer-identifiable placeholders."

Aisha responded, "That's handled. The agent runs in a secure on-prem environment. And we use regex-based redaction for test accounts. No customer data ever leaves the wall."

There was a beat of silence as that settled in. Suhani gave a short nod, the kind that said "I'd use that."

I turned the page in my notebook and added my notes:

- **AI augments human testers for efficient localization testing (web & mobile).**
- **Context-aware detection for localization issues with confidence scoring.**
- **False positives: Reduced through confidence scoring and manual review.**
- **Privacy concerns: Managed by using on-prem AI with redacted sensitive data.**
- **Model drift: Controlled via versioning, shadow mode testing, and cross-checking.**
- **Inconsistencies: Managed through output tagging, version control, and human QA.**
- **Engineering guardrails: Incorporated into CI/CD with manual review before deployment.**

- - -

By the time the final team returned to their seats, the air in the room had changed again. Like something had settled in us collectively. Possibility, maybe. Or just the quiet satisfaction that comes from showing your work and knowing it held.

I looked around at my team. Tired eyes, a few yawns, but no one had checked out. That meant something. This Hackathon was a glimpse into the future we might start building from now on.

And the ideas, god, the ideas.

There were too many to go deep on all of them, but a few still lingered at the edges of my notes:
A conversational AI to assist internal teams with globalization queries like "what's the date format for Korea?" or "how do we localize right-to-left UIs?" backed with the context you don't have to explicitly give, but can be gathered from the target application.
An LLM-driven glossary builder that suggests standard terms across domains using past translations and product taxonomy.
A script to auto-generate locale-aware placeholder content during development to prevent missing string errors in staging.
A plugin for Figma that uses AI to simulate translated layouts, testing for overflow, truncation, and mirroring issues before handoff.
A tone-shifting reviewer that flags overly literal translations and suggests regionally adapted, culturally attuned alternatives.
A Jira assistant that triages localization bugs, clustering by region, frequency, and potential revenue impact.

Some were just sketches. Others had the sharpness of something deployable. But all of them came from a place of care.
The possibilities with AI felt infinite. Gone were the days of cookie-cutter solutions, where we forced everything into one-size-fits-all models. AI has opened up the chance to tailor solutions to our specific needs, adapt to our internal processes, and even respect the nuances of our ever-growing product. The customization was no longer an afterthought, it was the starting point.

Two days of sprinting. Four weeks of quiet prep. Dozens of voices that rarely got to lead with their imagination.
I flipped to the final page of my notebook and wrote:
Next steps:
Set up check-in with Legal and InfoSec, AI governance alignment.

Schedule a post-mortem to gather feedback and refine the process.
Keep the momentum alive.

Across the room, Ava was already packing her laptop, a quiet smile tugging at her lips. This came from seeing something spark. She looked genuinely pleased, maybe even a little energized, as if the ideas had lit a fuse.
I caught her eye and nodded. She nodded back.

- - -

Vihaan sat hunched over the kitchen table, the paper in front of him almost mocking him. A few lines of a Sanskrit mantra, meant to be recited at the upcoming family event. Simple, right? But Ritu had insisted on the old-fashioned method: "Write it out 20 times," she'd said. "You'll remember it better."

To Vihaan, it felt like being sentenced to death by penmanship. "If this were on a computer," he muttered, "I'd just copy-paste it."
Kashika, who had been glued to her phone, looked up. "If it were me, I'd just let AI write it for me, and throw in some music."

We all chuckled, but Vihaan didn't. He just stared at the page, unmoving.
I leaned in. "The point isn't to fill the page, Vihaan. You're writing it to understand it. It's not about getting it over with. Writing it helps you remember. And reciting it... that's where the real work is."
Vihaan shot me a look. "Why are we still stuck with this old-school write-and-memorize routine? I could just play the mantra on my phone a few times, and I'd have it memorized in no time."

"And," I said, "you could ask AI to generate the audio that can be played in the event. Right? But will the guests enjoy the mantra the same way? If everything's AI-generated, where's the heart? Some things, like this, need the human touch. It's what makes it real. For that, you need to memorize it, understand it, and practice reciting with emotions."
Vihaan looked at me, his pen still hovering over the page, but I could see him thinking about it. Slowly, he began to write, his grip on the pen loosening as he started to engage with the words. There was still resistance, but I knew the repetition would work its magic.

Later, as the evening drifted toward quiet, I thought about the conversation. Vihaan had shown me how easy it was to overlook the value of the process. It was tempting to automate, to streamline, to do things faster. But some things, like mantras, like the human experience, needed to be felt, not generated.

That was where we were at work, too. The back-end, the invisible stuff, sure, that could be automated. But the things that mattered to the customers, those that talk to the customers, those need the human touch. You can't replace a person's engagement with a bot. Some things need to be done the old-fashioned way.

My Diary Notes

- Machine translation suits high-volume content; LLMs thrive in nuance.
- Control frameworks: prompt validation, caching, and human QA.
- Lock prompts and versions to minimize context gaps.
- Hallucinations happen, but human QA catches them.
- Engineering guardrails are a CI/CD checklist.
- LLMs aid code assessment, but humans remain in charge.
- On-prem work means balancing AI with privacy and security.
- AI augments engineers, never replaces them.
- Automation is fine, but the human touch is essential.
- Invisible tasks can be automated, but user-facing ones need humans.
- AI guides us, but we must steer it.

Chapter 12: Ethical Compass

Navigating the Grey Zones

May 19, 2024

The living room was unusually quiet for a Sunday afternoon. No clinking dishes. No phone calls. Just the voice of a debate host on YouTube, sharp and sure:

"The real question isn't whether AI can do it. It's whether it should."

I placed the folded laundry basket on the side table and walked in with a bowl of grapes, still a little warm from the rinse. The TV was playing a panel discussion, a livestream from some global summit. Four experts debated AI in public life, its reach into hiring, surveillance, and even education policy.

Kashika, legs tucked under a blanket, glanced at me. "Oh, you're done with the kitchen?"

"For now," I said, settling into the armchair beside them. My back was grateful.

Vihaan had spread his Lego pieces across half the coffee table. His head swiveled between his creation and the screen. "This guy talks like he's solving the world."

"Maybe he's trying to," Ritu murmured from the end of the couch, her tablet resting against her knees.

The room had the soft clatter of a family in weekend mode, half-thoughts, shared glances, and the occasional munch from a snack bowl. But the screen kept tugging everyone's attention.

"…facial recognition systems that work better on some races than others. The problem isn't only technical," the panelist continued, "it's that the teams building them didn't ask enough ethical questions early on."

That sentence hung for a while.

Then Kashika turned to me. "Papa, do the things you work on ever have ethical problems, too? Or is this just AI stuff?"

I looked at her. A straight, sincere question, curious, not confrontational.

And yet, I didn't have a straight answer.

Not because I suspected wrongdoing. But because I realized that we'd never explicitly asked. After we put the data governance framework in place, as I had discussed with Deepak on the flight, clarity followed. OKRs were no longer just tools for status updates; they had become central to our conversations. Each metric in the globalization tracker now had clear ownership, purpose, and a defined review cadence. But amid all these improvements, were we still operating within ethical boundaries?

That question lingered in the air, more alive than the debate we'd been watching.

I shifted forward in my chair and replied, "That's a good question. I'm not sure we've ever framed our work through that lens. But maybe we should have."

Ritu looked up, brows slightly raised.

I felt the stillness in the room solidify. We were no longer watching a conversation. We were in one.

Before anyone responded, I continued. "We work on how software reaches people across languages and cultures. That may sound harmless, or even helpful, but if we're careless, it can also go wrong."

"Like how?" Vihaan asked, genuinely curious.

Cultural Respect and Inclusion

"Let's say we launch a new feature that only works properly in English, and the translations for Spanish or Arabic are sloppy or delayed. Users in those regions might feel ignored, or worse, disrespected. That's one example."

"But isn't that just a bug?" Vihaan asked, tossing out the word with the ease of someone who'd clearly absorbed more from my work stories than I'd realized. I smiled at the fluency. He might not be in the industry, but he spoke like someone who'd been eavesdropping on my metaphors for years.

"Yes," I said, "but it's a bug that repeats. And when something keeps repeating, it stops being just technical, it starts to reflect how much a company values different people. That's where ethics begins to creep in."

Kashika frowned thoughtfully. "So, it's not about whether you meant to hurt someone, but about how they experience it."

"I would like to put it that way." I said. "Intent matters, but so does impact."

Ritu set her phone aside and joined in. "I read something recently… about how a calendar app launched with only

Sunday as the start of the week, and it confused people in the Middle East. It wasn't even a bug, just… a default."

"That's a perfect example," I said. "Defaults aren't neutral. They often reflect the worldview of whoever built the product or for whom the product was built for the first time. And when we apply them globally without pause, we quietly tell some people, 'This isn't really for you.'"

"So, how do you fix that?" Kashika asked. "Do you have to know every culture?"

"We try," I said. "We hire local experts, we ask native translators, and we build systems that allow for customization. But the challenge is when speed and scale get in the way."

Vihaan tilted his head. "So, if you're in a rush, you might forget to check?"

"It's not 'rush'. It's 'timing'. And it's not 'forget'," I said carefully. "But we might deprioritize. And that's the problem. When timelines tighten, whose experience do you choose to optimize first? That's an ethical choice."

There was a pause. The question hung in the air, heavier than I expected.

Equitable Experience Across Markets

Ritu broke it gently. "What about smaller languages? Do they get the same attention?"

I asked, "What do you mean by smaller languages?"

Ritu glanced toward me, her voice quieter but edged with curiosity. "Do you think your company gives equal weight to markets that *need* your solution, or mostly to the ones that *pay* for it?"

I paused, hearing the question that way stung a little. She wasn't accusing, just asking. Asking something that mattered.

She went on, gently. "I mean, I know you're not a nonprofit. But does that ever feel like a line you have to walk? Between doing what's good for business… and what's just *good*?"

I shook my head. "It's complicated. We focus on where the user base is large or revenue is high. That's the business logic. But it also means that some languages, spoken by millions, remain unsupported. That's not a technical limitation. It's a choice. A choice that has consequences."

Fair Market Practices

Ritu leaned forward. "And when you do go into these smaller markets, what happens to local businesses? Do they stand a chance?"

That landed like a pause in the room, not heavy, but thoughtful.

"It's something we have to be careful about," I admitted. "Global products, if not designed ethically, can end up displacing local solutions, ones that were serving their communities well before we showed up."

Ritu added, "At my NGO, we've seen it happen. A big global app comes in with better design and lower prices, and suddenly, the local service that supported five families shuts down, leaving them struggling for their livelihood."

Vihaan sat up. "That's like that movie we watched… where the burger company opens in a small town, and the little diner starts losing customers."
He squinted, thinking hard. "Ugh, what was it called? The one where the kid and his friends start a food truck?"

We all smiled.

"I know the one you mean," I said. "Even if we can't remember the name, the story's pretty clear."

Vihaan nodded. "Yeah. The big chain takes over, but the kid finds a way to fight back. I liked that."

"Wow," I said. "That's a great example. The big fish can easily swallow the small one if we're not careful."

Vihaan frowned. "That's not fair."

"It isn't," I agreed. "That's why fair market practices matter. Globalization should expand opportunity, not erase it."

Kashika tilted her head. "So, you're not just translating the product, but also making sure it doesn't destroy the ecosystem around it?"

"Yes," I said. "Sometimes that means partnering with local vendors. Other times, it means resisting the urge to offer deep discounts just to win a market. The goal is to build responsibly, not just quickly."

"So, to make them partners," Vihaan asked, "what do you do?"

"We give them a good experience," I replied. "Make it easy for them to join our ecosystem, whether they're vendors, delivery partners, or even setting up e-shops on our platform."

Kashika jumped in. "And you can't do that if they don't understand the system."

Cultural Respect and Inclusion

"Right," I said. "We can't ignore the languages or maybe the dialects they speak. If the onboarding experience assumes everyone's fluent in English or some metro language, we're quietly excluding a lot of potential."

Ritu added, "And not just excluding, perhaps ties to confidence, pride, and dignity."

Kashika leaned against the armrest. "If it were me, and something didn't work just because of my language, I'd feel invisible."

She looked at me and then at everyone else. "There's this group in my class, all from the same community. When they're just among themselves, they speak their own language. But the moment someone else walks up, someone who doesn't understand it, they switch to English. Even their jokes, their banter. They include everyone. No one even has to ask. It's just... how they are."

There was something powerful in what she'd said. A quiet reminder that inclusion isn't always about systems or features. Sometimes, it's just kindness made into a habit.

I nodded. "That's why we try to build in inclusivity. Not just patch it in after the fact."

Kashika tilted her head. "That explains how adding languages helps people feel included. But… maybe it's not enough? I mean, what about people who can't read the screen at all? You don't provide applications in Braille. Do you?"

That landed with quiet clarity.

I nodded. "You're right. Language inclusion is important, but inclusivity isn't complete if we ignore people with disabilities. We don't offer braille versions of our software, but we do make sure they work with screen readers, respond to voice commands, and follow accessibility standards. That's how we try to meet those needs."

I said. "You raised an important point, Kashika, because it's about fairness. Accessibility is an ethical responsibility. It ensures equal opportunity and respect for dignity."

Ritu added, "In my NGO, we saw whole groups left out because no one thought to make materials screen-reader friendly. When we retrofitted documents for screen readers in some communities, entire classrooms unlocked new learning."

I nodded. "That's why our work focuses on a few key ethical ideas when it comes to accessibility:

- Proactively removing barriers: We try to think ahead. Where might someone struggle to use this feature?
- Transparency and Communication: We clearly explain what's accessible and how.
- Addressing Bias: We check color contrasts, reading levels, and layouts so they don't unconsciously exclude anyone.
- Localized Accessibility: Even screen-reader instructions should be in the user's language.

Kashika and Vihan said, almost in unison, "That sounds interesting."

I nodded. "It is. It is interesting… and essential."

Data Privacy

Ritu glanced at the dining table's edge as if lining up a thought. "You know," she said, "at the NGO, we do have a few apps that are surprisingly accessible. Screen readers work well. But I've also noticed a hesitation, especially among older folks or those in vulnerable situations. They won't use e-commerce apps. Not because they can't navigate them, but because they're scared. Scared their card details will be stolen, or their data misused for ads, or worse."

I nodded, appreciating the direction this discussion was taking. "That's a very real concern, Ritu. Data privacy is central to the ethical framework of globalization. When we expand globally, we're not just looking at languages and currencies; we're also looking at how people's data is handled, how it's protected from misuse or exploitation."

Vihaan raised an eyebrow. "So, how do companies handle that? How do you make sure that people's private information is safe when you're scaling internationally?"

"Great question," I said. "It starts with data privacy laws and regulations. These laws give a lot of confidence to users that their data is secure and private. These laws vary from country to country. The laws might look similar in principle. They all emphasize protecting user privacy, preventing misuse, and ensuring transparency. But each country or region has its own specific requirements and nuances."

Ritu's eyes widened as she absorbed the details. "So, it's not just a one-size-fits-all solution?"

“No,” I continued, “and that's where the complexity of globalization comes in. For example, in the European Union, you have the General Data Protection Regulation, or GDPR, which mandates strict consent requirements and data handling practices. In California, there's the CCPA, which gives users more control over their personal data. Each law has its own set of rules about how long data can be retained, who can access it, and what to do if there's a breach.”

Kashika leaned in, intrigued. “But how does this work in real life, especially with applications and services that are used across different countries?”

“Well,” I said, “at ShopSphere, we take data privacy seriously. We ensure that we are compliant with these laws, no matter where our services are used. For instance, if someone in Europe accesses our platform, we make sure the data we collect is handled according to GDPR. If someone in California uses it, we ensure compliance with the CCPA.”

“But that's not enough,” I added, as I glanced at each of them. “Data privacy is about more than just following the law. It's also about respecting the users' right to privacy and being transparent with them. It's ensuring that when we collect data, we explain why we need it, how it will be used, and what rights the user has over their own information.”

Kashika nodded, clearly processing. “So, it's not just about what the law says, but also about earning trust.”

“True,” I said. “And here's where respect for the people in the pipeline comes in again. Just as we want to ensure that the people behind our translations and localized experiences are treated with respect, we must also respect the users' data. That means clear communication, consent, and taking the extra steps to ensure the data we collect is protected.”

Ritu added, "And if something goes wrong? How do you fix it?"

"Good question," I said. "That's why we have a robust system of transparency and traceability. If there's ever a breach or an issue, we need to know where it happened, who was responsible, and how we can fix it. But just as importantly, we must make it clear to our users who trust us with their data about what happened and how we're correcting it."

Respect for Labor in the Globalization Pipeline

Kashika leaned in; her expression thoughtful. "So, you're saying it's not just about fixing the problem but about knowing exactly where it happened and why?"

"Exactly," I said. "That's where accountability and observability come in. When you're dealing with multiple languages and regions, things can get complex fast. We need systems that are traceable, debug-friendly, and the ones that allow ethical auditing of localized experiences. If something goes wrong in one of the localized versions, we should be able to look at the logs and see which translation was used, who reviewed it, and when the issue first occurred."

Vihaan raised an eyebrow, clearly intrigued. "So, it's like having a map for everything?"

I nodded. "You can say that. It's all about having a clear path to follow. We can't just leave things to chance or hope the issue gets fixed on its own. We need dashboards and audit trails. These are the tools that help us trace back to the source of the problem. This isn't to blame. It's about understanding where something went wrong so we can correct it without wasting time."

“Hmm,” Kashika said, processing the idea. “So, having those logs lets you see what went wrong, but also helps you fix it faster?”

“Yes,” I replied. “The key here is veracity and fidelity. Veracity means that what we're presenting is truthful, not just in the original language, but also in how it's translated and localized. Fidelity means staying true to the original intent and meaning, no matter what language or culture we're adapting it for.”

Vihaan looked like he was connecting the dots. “And if you don't have those systems in place, how can you be sure what went wrong or how to fix it?”

“That's the risk,” I said, looking at him. “Without those systems, we're flying blind. If a translation is off, we might not know who reviewed it, or if it's an outdated version, or if something got lost in the translation. Worse, if we don't have those systems, it becomes impossible to fix problems quickly, which impacts both our ability to deliver quality experiences and the trust our users place in us.”

Ritu leaned back, clearly absorbing the weight of it all. “So, it's not just about fixing bugs. It's about having the right processes in place so that we can trust what we're delivering to users.”

I nodded. “And that's why accountability and observability are so important. When we trace back the work, we maintain transparency and trust with our users and within the team. It helps us continuously improve, stay aligned with our values, and make sure that every experience, every translation, and every piece of content stays true to our vision.”

- - -

The conversation had carried us through the afternoon, each of us mulling over ideas, some quiet, others more fervent, but the atmosphere in the room was easy, familiar. We'd never set out to solve the world's ethical problems, but somehow, by the time the debate on the screen had wrapped up, we had settled into a quiet understanding of our own. It was still a typical Sunday, one of those days where Vihaan was back to assembling his Lego structure, Kashika was lost in her book, and Ritu had returned to checking her messages. But there was an undercurrent now, a shared recognition that, while we had found some honest answers to our questions, we had also uncovered a truth that hadn't been clear before. So far, our work has been ethical by accident, guided by instinct and perhaps a sense of good intentions, but never by a defined ethical framework.

As the sunlight softened through the window, I felt a lingering sense of responsibility settle in. The conversation wasn't over, not really. We had our answers, but the bigger realization was that without an explicit focus on ethics in every decision, we might unknowingly slip. The day continued, but the weight of the moment remained, quietly shaping my thoughts as the Sunday unfolded around us.

That evening, I made a quiet note to myself: *we need to bring an ethical lens into our globalization work.* It was time.

My Diary Notes

- Ethical work is about design, not just accidental good intentions.
- Intent matters, but so does impact.
- Remember: Defaults are never neutral.
- Tight timelines often reveal our true ethical priorities.
- Globalization should expand opportunity, not erase it.
- True inclusion often begins with simple kindness.
- Accessibility is an ethical responsibility.
- Data privacy is more than law; it's about earning trust.
- Accountability and observability are key to ethical scaling.
- our work needs a defined ethical framework, not just good instincts.

Chapter 13: Bringing It All Together

A System That Globalizes on Demand and at Scale

Jul 8, 2024

The morning sunlight cut clean lines across the glass walls of the strategy room. The long oak table reflected soft glints off laptops and coffee mugs, but the room itself carried the charged stillness that only surfaced when big decisions were on the table.

Around the table sat the executive leadership team, Lorenzo, along with several of the company's VPs and senior strategists, focused, composed, and deliberate. Beside me, my own Core Globalization Team: Amira, Ava, Marco, Nina, Suhani, listened closely, their presence a quiet reinforcement of the expertise we had built.

Lorenzo opened the meeting, his tone measured but forward-leaning. "We're here today to discuss GlobaCart," he began, glancing at the agenda on the screen.
"Our acquisition talks have advanced significantly. The market opportunity is clear, their product complements our roadmap and expands our reach into several new regions."
He paused briefly, letting the business rationale settle before pivoting.
"But beyond market fit, there's something we need absolute clarity on, and that's system fit."

Several heads nodded around the table.

Lorenzo continued, “This is where I want your team's insight. The question we need to answer isn't simply, can we globalize GlobaCart? The question is, how smoothly and quickly can we integrate their product into the globalization engine we've built?”
He gestured subtly toward me, signaling it was time to speak.

I met his gaze, a quiet confidence rising, we had prepared for exactly this moment.

“We had spent months deliberately layering every part of this system, methodically, step by step.”

I paused before continuing, letting the weight of the moment breathe.

This wasn’t just about GlobaCart. This was about the system we had built. The system we had become.

We didn’t begin with answers. We began with questions. What assumptions had we made about language, about markets, about users whose contexts we barely understood? That first act, slowing down to assess, to confront our blind spots, changed us. It taught us that global readiness wasn’t a technical puzzle; it was a mindset shift. One that demanded clarity, honesty, and an appetite for change.

From there, we didn’t sprint. We mapped. We learned to separate noise from signal, to scope what was necessary and sequenced, not what was simply desirable. We embraced the discipline of phasing, starting where it mattered most, layering complexity only when the foundation could support it. That discipline stayed with us and now guides every integration we approach.

But systems don’t build themselves. People do. And the more we tried to centralize globalization into a role or a function, the more we realized it had to be shared. So, we invited everyone in. Product, design, QA, marketing, customer support. They weren't just consulted. They became accountable. We built bridges between teams that had once worked in silos, and suddenly the work wasn't just getting done, it was being understood.

We made it real. We named the roles. We gave someone the job of thinking globally, full-time. We brought in partners, but this time, we brought them in early, upstream. Not to rescue us after launch, but to build with us from the ground up. And we structured the chaos. We created plans with timelines and contingency paths, not just roadmaps with aspirations.

Along the way, we learned that not all bugs crash systems, some just confuse users. A missing plural rule, a mismatched gender, a poorly concatenated string. These weren't minor details. They were cracks in trust. So, we stopped treating translation as afterthought and began designing for expression, for grammar, for identity. Our engineering became linguistically aware. Our localization became a craft, not just a process.

Still, with every new locale and feature, we faced the same fear: what could break? That fear made us sharper. We invested in guardrails, for code, for content, for logic, for risks. We created a safety net that let us move faster without bracing for disaster. We built for resilience, not just for scale.

Then came the real evolution. We stopped globalizing features after the fact. We started thinking globally *by design*. Global readiness became a default expectation. Not something special, but something standard. Engineers knew the patterns. Designers asked the right questions. And every new product idea was vetted for scale before it left the whiteboard.

As we matured, we welcomed an outside view, fresh eyes that helped us see where familiarity had made us blind. What we built wasn't just good; it was inspectable. Observable. Repeatable. Localization wasn't magic. It was operational. And that shift, from intention to instrumentation, was what gave us the confidence to expand further.

We put systems behind the intuition. Real-time dashboards replaced hunches. We could see which languages were lagging, which vendors were overextended, which product flows were struggling with adaptation. Localization became live, measurable, and ultimately, improvable.

And just when we thought we had reached stability, the world shifted again. AI entered, not as a gimmick, but as a multiplier. We explored large language models for linguistic review, deployed autonomous testers across locales, and used AI-assisted tooling to analyze code for hidden i18n risks. But we did it with principles. We chose augmentation over replacement. Oversight over automation. Intelligence with accountability.

Now, sitting in this room, with a product like GlobaCart on the table, I no longer ask if we're ready.

I know we are.

Because readiness isn't just a checklist. It's a system of decisions. A culture of consideration. A discipline of doing the small things right, repeatedly, consistently, and intentionally.

We know how to begin. We know how to build. We know how to scale. And most importantly, we know how to learn.

We don't build global-ready products anymore.

We build systems that churn global-ready products.

This is what it means to be **Global by System**. Not reactive, not ad hoc, but deliberate, designed, and repeatable.

"Our system is mature. Technically, we should be able to integrate GlobaCart into our globalization cycle very quickly, far quicker than when we started with ShopSphere."

I paused, glancing around the room to let that confidence settle before continuing.

"However, just as we did when we began our globalization journey, we need to understand exactly where GlobaCart stands, its readiness, its gaps, and how well it aligns with the system we've built. Before we integrate, we must illuminate. I would recommend…"

I paused and glanced around the room to make sure everyone was listening.

"…that we start with an assessment."

- - -

The evening light spilled soft gold across the highway as I drove home, the quiet hum of the engine offering a rare pocket of stillness. The meeting had gone well, decisive, clear, and forward-looking, but it wasn't the strategy or the slides lingering most in my mind.

It was the journey.

When we first set out to build our globalization system, I had reached out to Naren, almost on instinct. Reconnecting with him had been more than a professional move; it had reopened a channel of trust and wisdom that had long shaped how I thought and led. His quiet guidance had framed much of the foundation we stood on now. What started as advice on processes had slowly turned into conversations about balance, growth, and perspective, lessons that echoed far beyond the office walls.

As the city lights blinked into view and the familiar turns of my neighborhood approached, I thought of home.
Of Ritu's calm steadiness, her quiet confidence that had always anchored me, no matter how turbulent the days became.
Of Kashika's bright curiosity and stories of her day, always eager to share something new.
And of Vihaan's laughter, quick, unfiltered, a reminder of how simple joy could be.

Somewhere along the line, as we architected a system capable of scaling globalization effortlessly across products, I had found my own life gently scaling towards balance as well.

We had built something that could grow and absorb, something resilient and repeatable.
And in doing so, I had rebuilt something within myself, something steady, rooted, and whole.

I turned into the driveway, headlights cutting a soft arc, and smiled.
We were ready, at work and at home, for whatever came next.

Epilogue

Looking back, I can see the outlines of what we did right, how intentionality, collaboration, and system thinking turned a sprawling challenge into a scalable capability. But I can also see where the edges frayed, where hindsight brings clarity that was hard-won.

We underestimated the value of early vendor engagement. LinguaLogic Partners had been instrumental in training and auditing, but I now realize they could have done so much more if brought in sooner, not just as external validators, but as strategic collaborators. We brought them in as a patch; they could've been a blueprint.

We also leaned heavily on internal instincts in the early phases, especially during team formation. While that built trust, it delayed the benefits we might've gained from broader perspectives, especially from those who had already walked similar paths in other global organizations. A stronger early alliance with seasoned globalization architects could have accelerated our foundation.

There were moments when we treated automation as an afterthought, building pipelines reactively rather than designing them into the architecture from the start. It took hard lessons and a few broken releases to learn that operational excellence in globalization isn't a bonus. It's the baseline.

Our LocOps maturity came late, too. If we had embedded localization deeper into our DevOps culture earlier, we would have avoided several painful misfires, especially around last-minute string changes and region-specific rollouts.

And when we finally introduced AI, it was a moment of momentum but also a lesson in humility. We saw its power. We also saw the critical need for thoughtful guardrails, human-in-the-loop practices, and well-defined scopes. AI didn't solve globalization. It elevated it when used wisely.

But even these missteps were part of the system's evolution. We learned. We adjusted. We didn't globalize by accident or by urgency. We globalized by design.

And that, in the end, is what matters most.

The journey taught us that being **Global by System** means more than building the right tools. It's about shaping the right behaviors, the right rhythms, the right questions. It's about knowing that scale isn't just what you reach for. It's what you prepare for, every step of the way.

We're not just ready for the next product.

We're ready for the next era: **Global by System**, by intentions, and by belief.

Appendix I: Internationalization (i18n) Grading System

Parameters and Rating Criteria

1. Externalized Texts

- **1 (Poor)**: All user-visible strings are hardcoded.
- **2 (Needs Improvement)**: Some strings are externalized, but many remain hardcoded or externalization is ad hoc.
- **3 (Average)**: All strings are externalized, but the method is basic (e.g., plain text files with no translation workflow).
- **4 (Good)**: Strings are externalized using a robust framework (e.g., ResourceBundle for Scala, gettext for Python) and integrated into a translation process.
- **5 (Excellent)**: Full externalization with translation workflows, context for translators, and support for dynamic updates.

2. Locale Support

- **1 (Poor)**: No locale support; application assumes a single language/region.
- **2 (Needs Improvement)**: Basic locale support, limited to one or two predefined locales.
- **3 (Average)**: Locale support is configurable, but fallback for unsupported locales is missing.
- **4 (Good)**: Comprehensive locale support with fallback mechanisms for missing translations or unsupported locales.
- **5 (Excellent)**: Dynamic locale management, covering a wide range of locales, including rare ones, and customizable by users.

3. Date, Time, and Number Formatting

- **1 (Poor)**: Formats are hardcoded and locale-agnostic.
- **2 (Needs Improvement)**: Formats are partially configurable but do not follow locale-specific rules.
- **3 (Average)**: Basic locale-sensitive formatting is implemented for common use cases.
- **4 (Good)**: Comprehensive formatting for dates, times, numbers, and currencies based on locale.
- **5 (Excellent)**: Customizable formatting with support for edge cases and cultural nuances.

4. Encoding Handling

- **1 (Poor)**: Application does not handle UTF-8 or non-ASCII characters correctly.
- **2 (Needs Improvement)**: Encoding issues occur with certain characters or languages.
- **3 (Average)**: Basic UTF-8 support, but occasional issues with special characters.
- **4 (Good)**: Reliable UTF-8 encoding and decoding for all supported locales.
- **5 (Excellent)**: Seamless encoding handling, including complex scripts and special symbols.

5. Language Fallbacks

- **1 (Poor)**: No fallback mechanism; application breaks for unsupported languages.
- **2 (Needs Improvement)**: Minimal fallback support, with limited functionality.
- **3 (Average)**: Fallback mechanism works for major languages but may miss edge cases.
- **4 (Good)**: Comprehensive fallback mechanism for unsupported locales.
- **5 (Excellent)**: Intelligent fallback system, covering language and regional variations.

6. Resource Management

- **1 (Poor)**: No organized resource management; texts are scattered.
- **2 (Needs Improvement)**: Some organization, but resources are not localized effectively.
- **3 (Average)**: Resources are centralized but lack flexibility for large-scale i18n.
- **4 (Good)**: Resource bundles or files are well-organized and locale-specific.
- **5 (Excellent)**: Efficient and scalable resource management with automated updates.

7. Pluralization

- **1 (Poor)**: No support for plural forms.
- **2 (Needs Improvement)**: Partial support for pluralization (e.g., English rules only).
- **3 (Average)**: Pluralization is supported for multiple languages, but with gaps.
- **4 (Good)**: Comprehensive pluralization support for a variety of languages.
- **5 (Excellent)**: Advanced pluralization, including edge cases and rules for complex languages.

8. Text Direction Support

- **1 (Poor)**: No support for RTL languages.
- **2 (Needs Improvement)**: Minimal RTL support, with layout issues.
- **3 (Average)**: Basic RTL support, but not seamless (e.g., mixed RTL and LTR content).
- **4 (Good)**: Full RTL support, including proper layout mirroring.
- **5 (Excellent)**: Seamless support for RTL and bidirectional text scenarios.

9. Collation and Sorting

- **1 (Poor):** Sorting is hardcoded and locale-agnostic.
- **2 (Needs Improvement):** Basic sorting for a single locale.
- **3 (Average):** Locale-sensitive sorting is implemented but limited to major languages.
- **4 (Good):** Comprehensive locale-sensitive sorting for multiple languages.
- **5 (Excellent):** Advanced collation and sorting, including custom rules for cultural nuances.

10. Dynamic Locale Switching

- **1 (Poor):** No ability to switch locales dynamically.
- **2 (Needs Improvement):** Locale can only be switched by restarting the application.
- **3 (Average):** Dynamic locale switching is supported but with delays or inconsistencies.
- **4 (Good):** Smooth dynamic locale switching with minor limitations.
- **5 (Excellent):** Instantaneous locale switching with consistent behavior.

11. Complex Scripts

- **1 (Poor):** Application does not support complex scripts (e.g., Chinese, Indic).
- **2 (Needs Improvement):** Minimal support for complex scripts, with rendering issues.
- **3 (Average):** Basic support for complex scripts, but layout issues remain.
- **4 (Good):** Comprehensive support for complex scripts.
- **5 (Excellent):** Seamless rendering and handling of complex scripts, including ligatures.

12. Text Expansion and Contraction

- **1 (Poor)**: No consideration for text length changes during translation.
- **2 (Needs Improvement)**: Minimal handling of text expansion, leading to layout issues.
- **3 (Average)**: Basic support for text length variations but occasional overflow.
- **4 (Good)**: Robust handling of text expansion/contraction across UI components.
- **5 (Excellent)**: Seamless handling of text variations, including dynamic resizing.

Instructions

1. Use the rating criteria above to grade each parameter for your Scala or Python service.
2. Assign a score (1-5) to each parameter based on its implementation quality.
3. Total the scores to assess overall i18n readiness. Optionally, assign weights to parameters based on priority for your use case.

Appendix II: Universal Design with Regional Flexibility

Key Considerations for Global User Interfaces

This reference sheet outlines key principles for designing globally consistent software interfaces while allowing necessary regional adaptations.

Design Aspect	Global Principle	Regional Flexibility Example
Navigation	Consistent navigation structure	Menu order adjusted for LTR/RTL scripts
Iconography	Universal, recognizable icons	Icons adapted for local symbolism
Name Fields	Standardized form structure	Field order swapped (First/Last vs Last/First)
Date & Time	Support ISO and global standards	Regional date formats and 12/24-hour clocks
Numbers & Currency	Locale-agnostic numeric inputs	Decimal separator (comma/period), currency symbol position

Colors	Neutral, accessible color palette	Avoid regionally sensitive colors
Address Fields	Comprehensive address components	Region-specific field labels and order
Layout Density	Balanced whitespace and information	Adjusted for minimalism vs content-rich layouts
Legal Notices	Baseline privacy and consent notices	Region-specific compliance (GDPR, CCPA, LGPD)
Sorting & Search	Logical search and sort behavior	Locale-specific collation (e.g., German ß, Japanese kana)
Measurement Units	Metric and imperial support	Locale-appropriate units
Text Expansion	Flexible UI components	Accommodate longer or shorter translations
Calendars & Holidays	Standard calendar system	Support for local calendars and public holidays
Phone Numbers	Standardized input pattern	Country codes and formats
Pluralization & Grammar	Grammatically correct UI text	Support complex plural forms and gendered language

Appendix III: Globalization & Localization Metrics

"What gets measured, gets governed, but only if what we measure is clear, owned, and used to improve."

This appendix provides a curated list of globalization and localization metrics.
For each, we explain **what it is, why it matters**, and **how to start measuring it**.

1. Translation & Linguistic Quality Metrics

- **Translation Coverage**

Measures the percentage of user-facing content translated into each target language.
Why it matters: Ensures feature and content parity across markets.
How to measure: Track total translatable strings versus translated strings in your TMS.

- **Translation Accuracy**

Assesses the linguistic quality of translations: grammar, spelling, and context fit.
Why it matters: Poor translations erode user trust and usability.
How to measure: Conduct manual linguistic QA or leverage automated grammar-checking tools.

- **Terminology Consistency**
  Ensures consistent use of approved product and brand terms across all translations.
  Why it matters: Protects brand identity and product clarity

globally.
How to measure: Perform glossary validation within your TMS or conduct random spot checks.

- **Style Guide Compliance**
  Checks if translations align with locale-specific style guidelines (tone, formality, etc.).
  Why it matters: Maintains culturally appropriate and on-brand communication.
  How to measure: Manual review by linguistic QA teams against defined style guides.

- **Post-Launch Locale Bug Rate/ Escaped Localization Bugs**
  Tracks the number of localization-related defects found after release.
  Why it matters: Reveals weak points in l10n QA and readiness processes.
  How to measure: Count localization issues in your issue tracker.

2. Internationalization (i18n) Quality Metrics

- **i18n Code Coverage**

  The percentage of code paths verified to comply with internationalization best practices.
  Why it matters: Highlights gaps in the codebase that could block globalization readiness.
  How to measure: Use static analysis tools or linters to detect non-compliant patterns (e.g., hardcoded strings, locale-naïve code). Integrate into CI/CD to auto-generate reports.

- **Hardcoded String Count**
  Counts the number of text strings embedded directly in the source code (not externalized).
  Why it matters: Hardcoded strings block translation and scalability.
  How to measure: Use static code analysis or search scripts (e.g., grep).

- **Concatenated String Count**
  Identifies text strings dynamically stitched together in code (e.g., `"Hello " + user`).
  Why it matters: Risks grammar issues and incorrect word order in other languages.
  How to measure: Scan code for concatenation patterns involving user-visible text.

- **Pseudo-localization Pass Rate**
  Measures how well the UI handles artificially "stretched" or accented text.
  Why it matters: Exposes i18n flaws (e.g., layout breaks, encoding issues) early.
  How to measure: Run automated tests with pseudo-locale strings and verify rendering.

- **Pluralization Handling**
  Assesses if plural forms are correctly implemented across languages.
  Why it matters: Prevents grammatically awkward or incorrect phrasing.
  How to measure: Validate plural rules using i18n

libraries like ICU MessageFormat.

- **Locale-aware Formatting**
  Checks if dates, times, numbers, and currencies are formatted correctly per locale.
  Why it matters: Enhances user familiarity and trust.
  How to measure: Test against standards (CLDR) or use Intl APIs in-app.

3. User Interface & Experience Metrics

- **String Truncation Count**
  Tracks how many UI elements cut off translated text.
  Why it matters: Poor usability and unprofessional UI.
  How to measure: Use automated scanning tools or manual UI QA.

- **BiDi (RTL) Support**
  Evaluates whether the UI properly supports right-to-left languages (Arabic, Hebrew).
  Why it matters: Enables key regional markets.
  How to measure: Test with RTL locales and verify mirrored layouts.

- **Font Coverage Score**
  Assesses if application fonts fully support all target scripts (e.g., Cyrillic, Devanagari).
  Why it matters: Prevents missing characters and broken text.
  How to measure: Render sample text in each script and visually verify.

- **Layout Adaptability Score**
 Measures how well the UI accommodates different text lengths and scripts.
 Why it matters: Prevents layout breaks and improves user experience.
 How to measure: QA test with longest translations and check responsive design.

- **Visual Regression Defect Count**
 Tracks UI layout or styling issues caused by localization changes.
 Why it matters: Maintains visual consistency and quality.
 How to measure: Use screenshot diffing tools during l10n QA.

4. Operational & Process Health Metrics

- **Automated Test Coverage by Locale**
 Measures the extent of automated tests executed in localized environments.
 Why it matters: Ensures localized builds don't introduce bugs.
 How to measure: Track test runs across locales in CI/CD pipelines.

- **Support Ticket Volume by Locale**
 Tracks user-raised issues segmented by language or region.
 Why it matters: Highlights friction points in specific markets.
 How to measure: Analyze customer support logs by

locale.

- **Market Content Readiness**
 Assesses how much of marketing, help, and support content is localized per region.
 Why it matters: Ensures complete go-to-market coverage.
 How to measure: Calculate localized content vs. master content counts.

- **Locale Launch Readiness Score**
 A composite metric showing how prepared a locale is for launch (content, QA, compliance).
 Why it matters: Aligns stakeholders on launch timelines and blockers.
 How to measure: Combine % translation complete, QA pass rates, and compliance checks.
- **Translation Velocity**

 The average time taken to complete translations from content handoff to delivery.
 Why it matters: Helps optimize localization workflows and accelerate time-to-market.
 How to measure: Track timestamps from handoff to translation delivery. Report average durations by language, content type, or release.

- **Translation Rework Rate**

 The percentage of translated content requiring rework or retranslation after review.

Why it matters: Reveals quality inefficiencies and upstream content clarity issues.
How to measure: Track rejected translations or major revisions in your TMS. Analyze trends and root causes.

5. Market Impact & Business Metrics

- **Cultural Appropriateness Score**
  Assesses if visuals, icons, references, and colors suit the target culture.
  Why it matters: Avoids cultural insensitivity and increases relevance.
  How to measure: Expert cultural reviews, user surveys, or SME audits.

- **Localized Search Relevance Score**
  Evaluates how well in-app search returns appropriate localized results.
  Why it matters: Improves discoverability and content access.
  How to measure: Test search queries in local languages and review outcomes.

- **Localized Conversion Rate**
  Measures the % of users completing desired actions in localized versions.
  Why it matters: Directly ties localization quality to business outcomes.
  How to measure: Segment analytics conversions by locale.

- **Bounce Rate per Locale**
  Tracks how quickly users leave the localized site/app.
  Why it matters: Identifies content or usability issues by market.
  How to measure: Analytics tool reports segmented by language/region.

- **Localized Onboarding Completion Rate**
  Measures the % of new users completing onboarding flows in localized versions.
  Why it matters: Critical for user retention and adoption.
  How to measure: Funnel tracking of onboarding journeys per locale.
- **Market-Specific Feature Adoption Rate**

  The percentage of users in a locale actively using a regionally targeted feature.
  Why it matters: Measures cultural resonance and informs feature prioritization by market.
  How to measure: Instrument product analytics to capture feature usage segmented by locale. Combine with regional user feedback.

- **Cost per Locale**

  The total localization-related cost (translation, engineering, QA) to support each locale.
  Why it matters: Enables ROI analysis and informed budget allocation by market.
  How to measure: Aggregate localization costs and allocate them by locale. Compare costs with revenue or usage metrics.

- **Global User Sentiment Score**

  The average customer satisfaction or NPS segmented by locale.
  Why it matters: Provides insights into localized user experience and satisfaction levels.
  How to measure: Embed locale-aware surveys or app ratings. Analyze sentiment trends by region.

6. Compliance, Payments & Infrastructure Metrics

- **Address Format Accuracy**
  Ensures support for locale-specific address formats and fields.
  Why it matters: Smooth checkout and user registration globally.
  How to measure: Form testing and validation against address schemas.

- **Payment Method Coverage**
  Assesses support for popular regional payment methods.
  Why it matters: Drives higher conversion in-market.
  How to measure: Audit available payment methods by region.

- **Regulatory Compliance Score**
  Tracks adherence to data privacy and regulatory laws (GDPR, LGPD, PIPL, etc.).

Why it matters: Mitigates legal and financial risk.
How to measure: Compliance checklists and legal audits.

7. Holistic Readiness Metrics

- **Global Readiness Index**
A composite score reflecting overall globalization maturity (i18n, l10n, UX, content, compliance).
Why it matters: Provides executives a high-level dashboard of global readiness.
How to measure: Weighted average of key metrics most relevant to your business.

How to Apply These Metrics

1. **Start small and prioritize**: Don't track all metrics. Focus on 4–6 aligned to your immediate goals.
2. **Assign clear ownership**: Embed metrics into existing team roles (as we discussed in the chapter).
3. **Visualize simply**: Dashboards beat spreadsheets; integrate with TMS, analytics, or Jira.

Iterate over time: Metrics should evolve as your globalization program scales.

Bibliography

- Doerr, John. *Measure What Matters: How Google, Bono, and the Gates Foundation Rock the World with OKRs*. Portfolio, 2018.
- Hubbard, Douglas W. *How to Measure Anything: Finding the Value of Intangibles in Business*. Wiley, 2014.
- Kim, W. Chan, and Mauborgne, Renée. *Blue Ocean Strategy: How to Create Uncontested Market Space and Make the Competition Irrelevant*. Harvard Business Review Press, 2015.
- Schlegel, Anna N. *Truly Global: The Theory and Practice of Bringing Your Company to International Markets*. Inkshares, 2016.
- Seiner, Robert S. *Non-Invasive Data Governance: The Path of Least Resistance and Greatest Success*. Technics Publications, 2014.
- Unicode Consortium. *ICU MessageFormat*. https://unicode-org.github.io/icu/userguide/format_parse/messages/
- Unicode Consortium. *Common Locale Data Repository (CLDR)*. https://cldr.unicode.org

www.ingramcontent.com/pod-product-compliance
Lightning Source LLC
LaVergne TN
LVHW090316210926
848480LV00001B/267
* 9 7 8 1 0 6 9 5 7 9 3 4 8 *